FREEDOM
FROM
ANXIETY

FREEDOM FROM ANXIETY

PAUL McKENNA DPhil

WELBECK

Published in 2023 by Welbeck
An imprint of Welbeck Non-Fiction Limited
Part of the Welbeck Publishing Group
Offices in: London – 20 Mortimer Street, London W1T 3JW &
Sydney – 205 Commonwealth Street, Surry Hills 2010
www.welbeckpublishing.com

A CIP catalogue record for this book is available from the British Library.

ISBN 978-1-80279-550-9

Illustrations by Ben Hasler
Typeset by Seagulls.net
Printed and bound by CPI Group (UK) Ltd, Croydon CR0 4YY

10 9 8 7 6 5 4 3 2 1

Contents

Important Notice

These pages contain powerful, scientific, physical and psychological techniques that will enable you to find freedom from feelings of anxiety and quickly create feelings of inner calm. But this book is only half of what you need.

The other half is a series of powerful audio techniques which will help you to reduce and eliminate unnecessary anxiety and create more emotional equilibrium and deep calm.

These can be found at
www.paulmckenna.com/downloads

Go now to the website and use the password: freedom123

You must use both, in conjunction with each other, to achieve optimum results.

For an index of all techniques in this book, turn to page 184.

Introduction

If I could give people just one ability from everything I've learned, it would be to switch off anxiety and go into a state of instant calm at will. That's because one of the greatest problems facing the world today is too much stress and worry.

Unlike my previous books, which are very much practical manuals, this one is different. I want to bring you into my world and share with you some of the amazing techniques created by eminent psychologists and other scientists I have worked with, along with my own journey through personal development and the insights I've gained and I live by.

This book is not just a manual. It is a *whole brain* learning system that is going to conquer your anxiety, reset any patterns of thought and behaviour that hold you back and empower you to create a richer world for yourself. It does this in a number of ways. The narrative of this book and the instructions in the exercises I will guide you through, talk directly to your conscious mind. Powerful visualisation processes and the hypnotic trance will also help to you reprogramme your unconscious mind.

I've tried and tested these methods, they have helped me, thousands of people I have worked with and even people that everyone else had given up on and who were deemed to be 'incurable'. So I know they can free you from anxiety and I will guide you every step of the way.

I have written this guide now because there is a psychological pandemic following the emergence of Covid-19, yet most people don't have the skills to deal with these feelings. Two chaotic years of lockdowns and disruption followed by economic turbulence, uncertainty and the horror of war has led to anxiety becoming the background theme to our lives. Millions of people have trained their brains to get good at quickly going to worst-case scenarios. Yet, a recent YouGov study revealed one fifth of people with anxiety issues have no coping strategy.

With this tsunami of worry has come all of the physical and psychological effects you would expect to see associated with it, including depression, insomnia, bad or low mood, as well as mental blocks to people fulfilling their true potential. The super powerful scientific, physical, psychological and spiritual techniques in this book, which I have spent decades researching, are an antidote to that.

They are used by some of the world's leading doctors and scientists to heal anxiety, trauma, stress, phobias, PTSD and panic attacks. The results are astounding, fast and long lasting. This practical and personal guide and the accompanying audio I have specially created to go with it is a smorgasbord of approaches that will perform a reset of your brain, teach you how to become the master of your emotions and enable you to instantly access a sense of happiness, bliss and creativity too.

You may find that after the very first technique, you'll start to feel better, but don't worry if not, as each technique builds on the one before. So, whether you start to notice positive changes straightaway, or whether it takes you a few techniques, you'll find that the changes happen at the appropriate speed for you. You don't have to do it all at once. You can dip in and out of the audio and the book, as while the trance and each technique are individually effective, when you stack them together you can experience cumulative benefits. They will help you to reach an optimum state of mind, where you can see opportunities everywhere, be resilient and optimistic.

Our body's defence mechanism

Anxiety, fear, panic, stress and worry are all part of our protection mechanism that keeps us safe. I use these words interchangeably in this book as each is a product of our fight or flight response, that we inherited from our ancestors to either fight another animal or caveman, or run away.

An ancient part of the brain called the amygdala is where we process feelings of threat and fear – it is like your brain's ever-vigilant security guard. When it notices threats, or even potential threats, to yourself or your ego, it is triggered into action. When that happens, we produce a massive amount of lactic acid, adrenaline, blood is pumped to the limbs, the digestive system is halted and the immune system is affected so you can put everything you have got into either fighting or fleeing. That was very useful centuries ago in that it helped us to survive when someone – or something – wanted to kill us or eat us.

In our modern society, it gets triggered way too often unnecessarily. This means all day long, your fight or flight mechanism is mis-firing to a small or large degree. If you are cut up in traffic, miss the bus or train, are late for work, or get caught up in an argument, all of these things individually set it off over and over again. Even just *thinking* about something stressful can set it going. When your mind and body's protection mechanism is being constantly over-stimulated, it is not good for us. For many people, it's like an internal car alarm that's going off all the time and you don't have a way to stop it.

When you add into this mix the uncertainty of a global pandemic, you have the perfect storm. We know from studies of what people are most frightened of, 'The Unknown' is always in the top 10 and sometimes ranks even higher than death. One of the greatest ironies is because people are over-stimulating their fight or flight defence mechanism so much, they are more likely to be damaged by it, than saved by it!

In addition, when the threat detection mechanism over-signals in a social setting it can lead us to imagine other people are judging us or cause us to never want to step out of our comfort zone 'just in case' – leading to social anxiety. Latest figures estimate more than one in 10 people in the UK may suffer from social anxiety at some point in their lives.

We are also in a world where people are increasingly taking drugs for anxiety. Some people undoubtedly need these medications, but the people prescribing them often see medication as the only choice. It's a bit like if all you have is a hammer, then, everything looks like a nail. Because more and more people have been medicated for psychological problems since the '80s, you would think the issues would reduce, but actually they have got worse.

You'd think that maybe therapy would be another solution but some therapists want to *analyse and explain* everything rather than *concentrating on positive change*. That means when it comes to helping people all over the world, I've found many people have been through some kind of therapy and are able to tell me lots of reasons *why* they are anxious, or *why* they are stressed, but that hasn't enabled them to overcome it.

The good news is the answer to the problem really is very simple – and I'm going to show you step by step how to reduce your anxiety and have a calmer, more confident life.

The worry in anxious people's brains is over-doing its job and the techniques in this book and the audio downloads are going to reset it so that the stress signals less often and quieter in the background. That will, in turn, enable you to find balance – where you are comfortably aware of problems and potential issues and can think creatively to solve them. That will put you in great shape, and able to fully enjoy life.

Why is it good for you
to overcome anxiety?

If you think of yourself as an anxious person, I want to tell you something really important:

You are not bad, or broken, you have just picked up a few unwanted habits in your thinking and behaviour and everyone in the world has done that at some time.

Anxiety is exhausting. If you are constantly in a state of high alert and dread you will eventually overreact to everything and ultimately you will make mistakes, bad decisions and it can even lead to burn out. It also means you never get to really enjoy life.

One of the problems anxious people have is that they can't imagine life completely without worry and even the thought of reducing it means letting their guard down – leading them to get more anxious! When people are stuck in this state of mind, they can't think themselves out of it, they go round and round in ever decreasing circles until they are emotionally spent. That's because the unconscious mind is not logical, it's purposeful, and its purpose is survival. So together we are going to re-programme your mind, just like a computer.

My objective is not to completely take away your ability to get stressed, as from time to time you will need it. For instance, if your house is on fire, you need it to get you out of danger and stay alive. If you don't have any ability to get worried, you could just sit happily watching TV while a catastrophe strikes all around you.

There is also a positive side to stress, which can give you a competitive edge, and which is motivational and exciting. In some cases it can even be pleasurable – some people love the adrenaline rush of a bungee jump, while others like to be frightened out of their wits watching a good movie, or the rush of performing to an audience, or winning at sport.

So some situations require stress, but the secret is to be able to control it, so that you are the major shareholder in your own mind and body. When you can control when you do something you have *choice*. When you have choice you have *freedom*.

So while you may have been labelled as a particular type of person, in reality, you just learned some unhelpful ways of thinking and acting. In the few hours it takes to read this book, practise the techniques and listen to the audio you will start to feel more and more in control of your life and may start to wonder what you were worrying about. I've done this with thousands of people over the last decade and honed this programme to contain the most powerful techniques I know that will start to work right away.

Very often, when I'm working with an anxious person, they are sceptical and wonder if the techniques will work. However, as they stay with the process and keep using them, they always start to see results.

It can also help if you 'set your mind' to do it. Over the years I have had people say to me, for example, they have tried pretty much everything to stop a habit like smoking and it didn't work. When I asked them if they had ever stopped and just smoked immediately after a hypnotherapy session, they usually say something like: "No, I stopped for a few weeks." To which I say, if you can stop for a few weeks, you can stop for a few months and if you can stop for a few months, you can stop for a few years.

One patient I treated for insomnia came back to see me two weeks later and told me: "I'm not cured." I asked him how much better he was and he replied: "Only 80 per cent." I looked at him and said: "Listen to yourself!" At which point he realised he was looking for failure not success – for what he *hadn't* achieved, rather than what he *had*.

So, when people say to me: "Nothing's worked for me in the past" my advice is: "Just give it a chance." As you read this book and do the techniques, constantly notice your progress to see how well you're doing.

Moving towards a reset

Everyone experiences anxiety at some point. However, people who consider they are 'an anxious person' have made it a part of their identity. The NHS describes anxiety as a "feeling of unease, such as worry or fear that can be mild or severe".

From the moment they wake up anxious people overthink, worry about problems (both big and small), imagine scenarios that could occur, and they run them over and over in their minds until they become catastrophes. Fifty per cent of the reasons why people go to their doctor are stress related, or can usually be traced back to it in some way.

During the pandemic, we had disruption to the status quo all over the world, this created stress on a scale never seen before – it was literally in the global psyche.

One of the greatest ironies is that anxious people are often very organised and conscientious because all their energy goes into stopping problems and controlling as many things as possible. Many are also perfectionists.

In one respect, the world needs anxious people because they help to keep things running smoothly. However, they often do this at the expense of their health and the quality of their lives. Although thinking about potential problems is a good survival strategy, excessive stressful thoughts are harmful to long-term health and stop people from experiencing the full joys of life.

Many people also self-medicate with substances such as alcohol, drugs or smoking, as anxiety and stress fuel addiction, but, of course, it is possible to break this self-destructive cycle.

So, as the first step, I'd like to make a distinction. Concern, preparation, anticipating potential problems and heading them off at the pass are functional ways of thinking and acting. Anxiety is different. If you worry from the moment you wake up and can't relax because you believe that if you do, somehow you will miss something and it feels like the end of the world, or if you can't switch off, then you are suffering from anxiety.

If you're continually running catastrophic movies in your mind, or have a constant feeling of foreboding and a knot in the pit of your stomach, if even when things are going fine you still worry, because you tell yourself it won't last and catastrophe might be just around the corner, then that's real anxiety too.

If your quest for perfection drives you to high standards but you don't ever get to enjoy it as you are always looking for faults so that you could make it *even more* perfect then that is also anxiety.

But that is about to change. Remember, as you follow my instructions and listen to the audio techniques, you will soon find it easier to relax and as the landscape of your brain chemistry changes and a new default setting is established – you will have all your protection mechanisms in place, but they will not be on high alert all the time.

As I guide you every step of the way through this book and the accompanying audio, the majority of people will find they get significant results. On some people it may have an instant impact, while others may need to do the techniques multiple times to reinforce their success, but most people who use this system, will get a reset.

I recently helped a lady who had stress and anxiety etched on her face. She gripped the chair with white knuckles and the emotion in her voice told me how overwhelmed she was. At first, she found it difficult to relax, so I used every technique that I've put in Section One of this book and then suddenly, her muscles softened, her tone of voice relaxed and I could see that her racing mind began to slow down. At the end of the session, she said, "I feel so much better! It's like a weight off my shoulders!"

Afterwards I wondered which particular technique worked. I came to the conclusion it was the combination of all of them.

Why does this system work so well?

People often tell me, "I've got to have a holiday. I've just got to get away from all this stress!" and, yes, you can jet off and leave it behind you for a while, but when you come back, it'll be there waiting for you.

This system is about training your brain to create new perceptual filters, so that whatever stress is going on in your life, you are in a more resourceful place to deal with it. You won't have to jet off to escape your problems, you'll be able to make yourself calm and focused – wherever you are.

To achieve it, this book is split into three parts.

Section One focuses on *immediate relief from anxiety* using deceptively simple but stunningly effective Psycho-Sensory and Neuro-Linguistic Programming (NLP) exercises – where touch and visualisation transform the way you feel.

Section Two is a series of powerful psychological techniques, including self-hypnosis and more NLP to *build calm, resilience and boost good feelings.*

Section Three helps you to *create a richer world for yourself* using a number of practices in the realm of human potential. As once you have your stress and anxiety under control, you'll have more bandwidth in your thinking and feeling for optimism, joy and creativity.

Don't be too surprised at how well this works

It's fine to be sceptical – I'm a sceptical person, I like to test things and try them out before I decide how well they work. Many of the techniques in this book were once considered 'alternative' but are now becoming a part of the mainstream. The key thing is, even if you think it sounds far-fetched or strange, please follow all of the instructions and just give it a go.

For many years, hypnosis was treated as a dark art and not the widely accepted scientific technique for personal change that it is today. The early pioneers faced endless accusations of being charlatans.

Franz Mesmer created the forerunner to modern hypnosis, which was called 'mesmerism', and paved the way for it to be used in healing, yet he was publicly accused of being a fraud.

Dr James Esdaile, a nineteenth-century Scottish surgeon, did hundreds of operations using hypnosis as the only anaesthetic (he also invented the stethoscope). Many of his techniques are still used in hypnotherapy today, yet he was ridiculed for it, even though he was a brilliant man.

In modern times, psychiatrist Milton Erickson was widely regarded in the Seventies as the greatest hypnotist in the world. Yet, at one point, the medical authorities tried to take his medical licence away as he was so controversial. People who have been pioneers or disruptors are often not thanked for it at the time and only later seen as visionaries.

Mastering your thoughts and emotions

Most of us don't realise just how much control we can have over our thoughts and feelings, as we are not taught this at school. We are taught *what* to think, not *how* to think. The mind and body are linked in a cybernetic loop – in other words, one is always influencing the other. If you have stressful thoughts about catastrophes, that will alter your body chemistry and, in turn, change your physiology so your muscles will tense up. In contrast, when you have relaxing thoughts and say, think about going on holiday or remember a time when you were on the beach or by a pool, that also changes your feelings, body chemistry and it relaxes your physiology. All day long, our mind and body are in a dance, as it were, where one is influencing the other.

Research also shows that nearly half of what people do every day is just a habit. And some of that is really good – for instance, you don't have to think: "Shall I tie my shoe-laces?" or "Shall I get dressed?" – we just do it habitually. However, a lot of people also spend their lives living in hope that calm feelings will just magically show up.

Embracing calm and taking charge of your life

Since the pandemic, obtaining a work/life balance has moved up our list of priorities. A global survey done by IPSOS of more than 21,000 adults in 27 countries in September 2020 revealed seven in 10 people around the world wanted their life to change significantly rather than returning to how it was before the Covid-19 crisis. So, if there's anything positive that has come from this pandemic, it has been the fact that people have had a chance to think about what their priorities are.

But, it's no use just wishing that will magically happen. We have to think about *what* we want and acknowledge it every time we notice or experience anything that makes us feel happy. This reinforces abundance in the subconscious and opens our minds and eyes to opportunity that is all around us. Have you ever thought about, say, buying a particular car and then suddenly you see that make of car everywhere? You have subconsciously set up a filter to see it, whereas in the past you would have probably missed it. In the same way, when you are in a positive state, the world looks good, you start to see opportunities and you are fun to be around – and so you get more of the good stuff.

Over the years, I have spent time with miserable overachievers and millionaires who spend their lives chasing more and more status, power and money. They didn't really have much time with their family, and, more often than not, their health suffered. I'll never forget asking one person: "When you look into the future, what do you see?" He replied, "I'll have a bigger house, a yacht and a fleet of supercars" and I said, "Where are you in that picture?" He replied, "I can't see myself." And I answered, "So you are going to work yourself to death to get all of this?" There is a Japanese word called 'Karoshi', which literally means working yourself to death. There is also a book by Maria Nemeth called *The Energy Of Money* that describes it as: 'Busyholism'. This sums up a lifestyle where people feel the need to work all the time because they 'need the money' or 'can't bear to be bored' – but often they are actually addicted to the buzz they get from chemicals produced as a stress response. I could see the cogs in his mind beginning to turn when I raised this with him and he started to re-prioritise. It's really important that whenever you look into the future you envisage yourself healthy and happy – as that makes it more likely to become your reality.

When I was younger, I spent too much time moving away from fear of failure, rather than moving towards happiness and equilibrium. When I embraced the techniques we are about to do, the stress I'd felt for years first thing in the morning – due to my 'over achiever' mind-set vanished. I felt an overwhelming relief – I was no longer beating myself up that I was not working hard enough… conquering the world. Instead, I felt better – and crucially happier – than I had done in years.

One of my favourite quotes is from Holocaust survivor and psychiatrist Viktor Frankl, who said: "Purpose is the cornerstone of good mental health." Historically, people with the highest lifetime expectancy are from the island of Okinawa in Japan where there is an inscribed stone that roughly translated says: "At 80 you are merely a youth. At 90, if your ancestors invite you into heaven, ask them to wait until you are 100 – then you might consider it." Scientists have been studying longevity there since 1975.

There is plenty to be learned from the Okinawa way of life. Their secret is partly genetics and diet but also what they call your 'reason for being' *or 'Ikigai'*.

If you are anxious, your sole purpose is survival. When the volume has been turned down on anxiety, or it's gone, you have more room to find other things that you can enjoy in life. That could be becoming financially independent, creating something that helps lots of people or it could be something as simple as being a good friend, caring for your pet or doing random acts of kindness.

This book will guide you to explore all the opportunities you really want so you can enjoy a greater sense of mental and spiritual purpose and, in turn, a greater sense of joy and fulfilment. So let's put it into action.

Section One

Instant Freedom From Anxiety

This chapter is going to focus on 'fast fixes' for anxious feelings. Each of them take just minutes to work – and they can have a lasting impact.

Over the last 10 years, I have devoted a significant part of my life to working with people suffering from anxiety, extreme trauma, PTSD, depression and panic attacks. I have successfully treated war veterans, victims of rape, and people that have tried every technique and medication to recover from the terrible things they've experienced yet felt the system had given up on them.

Many of those I've met, including the soldiers, paramedics, firefighters and police officers, have put themselves in harm's way to protect or rescue others. Most felt they'd been dismissed as 'untreatable', were convinced that nothing was going to work, which compounded their problems, yet they have had their lives transformed by a combination of all of the following techniques in this chapter.

Scientific research has shown these techniques are amazingly successful in the treatment of anxiety disorders. They have only very recently started to become super popular. Many people find they work immediately, for others it takes a bit longer. Each method builds on the one before.

I'm always honoured when people endorse my work publicly and amongst the people who have spoken about using some of the techniques featured in this book are Hollywood icon Daryl Hannah who appeared on US TV saying I'd given her more confidence before going on stage, singer songwriter Sophie Ellis-Bextor who wrote in her biography how I helped her panic attacks and James Corden, who publicly thanked me for reducing his stress before he hosted the BRIT Awards. So no matter what your walk of life is, or why anxiety is affecting you – this system can make a huge difference.

First, I'd like to introduce you to a beautiful technique called Freeze Frame, which is used to reduce feelings of stress and overwhelm instantly.

The institute of HeartMath

Anxious people often want something they can do when they are feeling anxious 'there and then' to stop it. They want something to interrupt and reduce feelings of overwhelm and give them a sense of peace, calm, and feeling in control.

Freeze Frame does just that – it's an instant fix. It was created by the HeartMath Institute, which was set up in the early '90s to study the role of the physical heart in health and wellbeing. It has been taken up around the world, including by all four branches of the US military. So when people are in battle trauma or stress they can use this to reset themselves 'in the moment'.

The Institute discovered that actively focusing on the physical heart measurably reduced the presence of stress hormones, increased anti-ageing hormone levels, and enabled peak performance in a wide range of situations. They have developed a number of tools that are all built around one basic idea: when you shift your attention from your head to your heart, your body relaxes, your mind gets clearer, and your brain releases positive chemical changes of natural relaxation.

Lieutenant General Sir Graeme Lamb, the former director of the UK Special Forces and director of the British Field Army, once gave me a great metaphor of the effect that anxiety and stress has on the human body that perfectly illustrates this. He told me that, "Some military helicopters allow the pilot to override safety protocols in an emergency by increasing power above safe operating norms by over stressing the engines providing greater power. While this can save you from an immediate crisis, if the engines are allowed to run on, you replace the first problem with the very real possibility of a catastrophic engine failure and an inevitable crash landing."

Exactly the same can be said for the human body – it can cope in short bursts, but it cannot, without negative health consequences, be exposed to unrelenting stress and anxiety.

I taught Freeze Frame to a high-powered American lawyer who would come out of a courtroom, fired up on adrenaline. In order to calm herself down, she'd immediately eat a huge pizza. She was using food to medicate her state. After working with me, when she came out of court, all cranked up, before she ate anything, she did the technique. This meant she could calm herself down quickly without having to inhale a pizza to change her emotions.

You can use Freeze Frame any time you are experiencing stress in your body or your mind. It will help you to feel better almost immediately – usually in less than a minute. In addition, you may get insights into what to do to make things more the way you want them.

THE FREEZE FRAME TECHNIQUE

🔊 *You can download this audio technique now.*

Read through this technique several times first
and practise the whole sequence as many times as
you wish until you know you have memorised it
well enough that it is almost automatic when you
actually need to use it.

First of all, check how your anxiety level is on a
scale of one to 10.

1   Become aware that you are experiencing a
stressful feeling in your body or that your
mind is racing.

2   Put your hand on your heart and focus your
energy into this area. Take at least three
slow and gentle breaths into your heart,
maintaining your focus on the feeling of your
hand in the centre of your chest.

3   Now, recall a time when you felt really, really
    good – a time you felt love, joy or
    real happiness! Return to that memory as
    if you are back there again right now.
    See what you saw, hear what you heard, and
    feel how good you felt.

4   As you feel this good feeling in your body,
    imagine your heart could speak to you.
    Ask your heart how you could take better
    care of yourself in this moment and in this
    situation.

5   Listen to what your heart says in answer
    to your question and act on it as soon as
    you can.

Notice how well this has worked for you as many people
feel the difference instantly.

The role of destiny in this book

More than 20 years ago, a friend of mine raved about a psychic reading that she'd had. She was a psychologist and was very sceptical but had gone for one for fun and was blown away. So, after such a five-star review, I decided to visit the same psychic. As I walked in, she was sitting at a small table with a neatly stacked Tarot Card deck, some crystals in front of her and a bookcase with dozens of publications on it. Gesturing for me to take a seat, she reached round behind her and pulled out a book and handed it to me saying: "This is for you." I said: "Oh, thanks," thinking "Oh, here we go, what's this?" To my amazement she said: "No, you don't understand. *This* is for you, this is really important. You must read it." The title was: *Tapping The Healer Within* by Dr Roger Callahan. Puzzled, I asked: "Why is this important?" She was emphatic in her reply: "You are going to do important work with this man." If I'm completely honest, I was thinking, "This sounds like a load of nonsense." But she was so insistent I said: "OK, I'll read it."

The following day, I had to fly to New York and seeing it out on the table, at the last minute, I put it into my hand luggage. A few hours into the flight, I thought I might as well give it a look. Dr Callahan discovered that tapping in a specific way on key acupuncture points of the body has a rapid, reliable and predictable effect on our feelings and he called it Thought Field Therapy. His description of it is: "What TFT does is provide a code for eliminating emotional distress at its root cause." I had spent years learning hypnosis, NLP and psychology and frankly, at first, I didn't believe a word of it.

Then the person I was travelling with said: "I'm really dying for some chocolate," but she didn't want any, as she was on a diet. Coincidentally, I had just turned to the page on eliminating compulsions. So, because I had nothing better to do, I decided to try his compulsion busting technique on her. I asked: "On a scale of one to 10, how much do you want chocolate?" And she said: "10!" So, I told her: "Try this," and I went through the tapping sequence. She looked at me as if I had gone completely barmy. After she followed the instructions, I asked: "Where's the desire right now?" Her astonishing reply was: "It's completely gone!" I was blown away. I thought: "I need to test this again."

Across the aisle, a fellow passenger had been gripping her seat with white knuckles since boarding. I said: "Excuse me, madam, are you a nervous flyer?" She nodded. I said:

"Would you like to try a new technique to help you feel calmer?"

She nodded and I showed her the points to tap on. In just a few minutes, she said: "I'm not frightened! Oh, my word, it's gone!" There are times in our lives when you reflect back on past events and you realise the exact moment the trajectory of your life changed. This was one of them.

A few days later, I shared what had happened with NLP co-creator Dr Richard Bandler, who happened to know Dr Callahan, so we all went out for dinner. Dr Callahan had come from a conventional psychological background, taken a lot of knocks, criticism and even ridicule about his technique, but was quietly emphatic in the fact that it worked. He revealed it was so successful he cured all his patients in a matter of weeks and almost wiped out his practice – a victim of his own success!

TFT looks a little unusual, but many scientific studies show that it's amazingly effective at reducing stress, anxiety, trauma, addictive urges, depression, compulsion, phobias, panic attacks – and even a broken heart. His breakthrough brings together a modern scientific approach and the ancient understanding of the originators of acupuncture.

People initially dismissed his incredible breakthrough – which was a radical departure from traditional psychological treatments – as a distraction, nonsense and even a placebo. Yet, he had an excellent comeback to this. He said: "It can't be a placebo, as a placebo works when you are convinced it's going to. You take the pill as you think it's going to heal you and it's your belief that does it. But no, with this it is quite the opposite. People absolutely do *not* believe that tapping on a particular part of their body is going to create such a dramatic change." I'd like to share this powerful technique with you now.

Tapping into calm feelings

While Freeze Frame is a super quick 'in the field' interrupt, TFT is more sophisticated and is part of a family
of psycho-sensory therapies. For many people this technique, which is also referred to as 'Tapping', is their 'go to'
when they are feeling anxious or panicked due to a specific
problem. It takes a bit of practice to learn the sequence
but research irrefutably shows that it works incredibly
well on tackling anxiety.

Up until recently, the techniques and methods that traditional therapists used were very limited. For example,
psychoanalysis often takes a long time, is uncomfortable
and very expensive, which over decades, understandably led
to people having little faith in talking therapies. The problem with old-fashioned analysts is they get their patients to
relive all the worst things that have ever happened to them,
in the hope they will make a new judgement about the
trauma and, through realisation, be free of the traumatic
feelings. However, we now know this approach can *reinforce*
a trauma. What actually sets you free, is the *re-coding* of a
trauma – and that's how Thought Field Therapy works.

The word 'thought' in Thought Field Therapy in simplified terms refers to a specific memory or thought. Depending on what you are thinking about, your body will produce a physical response by secreting chemicals and hormones and sending electrical impulses that change the way you feel. The concept of 'field' relates to the fact *because you can't see, feel or hear something, doesn't mean that it isn't there.* The Victorian scientist Michael Faraday had an excellent example of this with his discovery that although our senses can't detect an electromagnetic field, it exists because if we place iron filings onto a piece of paper with a magnet underneath it, they move.

This technique is not merely a distraction. Scientific studies have shown that when we use the tapping technique in TFT we reduce stress chemicals in our body and produce states of relaxation and calm. We also change the way our brain processes thoughts and feelings. The effect of tapping in the specific sequence I will share with you is to reset the way that your brain interprets and responds to stress, thereby altering your internal brain structure.

TFT is also really effective for anxiety and phobias. All phobias and feelings of anxiety have a *positive* intent. So, if you get bitten by a dog or mistreated by a dentist or get stuck in an elevator, your mind decides to create a protection mechanism so, if any time in the future we experience anything that reminds us of that original incident, our fight-or-flight response is triggered to protect us. The sound of a dog barking, the smell of the dentist's office, the image of some lift doors closing can bring back the fear of the original incident. Remember, its intent is *positive* – it's just over-doing its job.

I have done TFT with the former queen of US TV Ellen DeGeneres live on her show and with the entire audience. I got them to think about something that upset or distressed them and then I asked them all to tap on the TFT points to reduce the stress and anxiety. After we'd done it for a few minutes, I asked: "Hands up who is no longer upset or stressed?" and nearly all of the hands raised – and that's what can be achieved with TFT, in just minutes, on television.

TFT can also mitigate the agony of bereavement, in some cases, almost instantly. When I first started practising TFT, I was doing an hour-long phone-in on Australian radio. Five minutes from the end, the final caller came on and said: "My wife has just died, my heart is broken and I can't get over it, please help me." I thought: "How am I going to do anything in just minutes?" So, I said: "I don't know how much I can reduce the pain, but I think I can help you mitigate it to an extent. I told him to tap the various points on his body to do with emotional overwhelm. Even though his grief was at a 10 when I started, within minutes I got it down to a four. That is its extraordinary power.

TFT isn't designed to cancel all feelings of upset because part of your emotional intelligence is to experience the full spectrum of emotions. I remember helping another man who was also suffering bereavement and whose emotions were so raw he said: "Can't you just take it all away?" I explained that as it had only just happened, I wouldn't be able to remove it all, as the grieving process needs to take place, but what I could do is mitigate it, so it wasn't so over-whelming and he could deal with his day-to-day life. So, he followed the protocol and just a few minutes later, he admitted: "You know, I actually do feel calmer, I don't feel so overwhelmed, I can sort of handle it."

Let me guide you through it now.

THOUGHT FIELD THERAPY

🔊 *You can download this audio technique now.*

Please read through the following exercise before you do it. After you have practised this tapping sequence several times, you will know it off by heart.

Before you start, just notice how much stress you feel. I'd like you to rate your stress on a scale of one to 10, with one being the lowest and 10 being the highest. This is important, because in a moment we want to know how much you've reduced it.

Now, take two fingers of either hand and tap about 10 times on the following points on your body, while you continue to concentrate on the unhappy feeling:

Tap the side of your hand (the karate chop point).

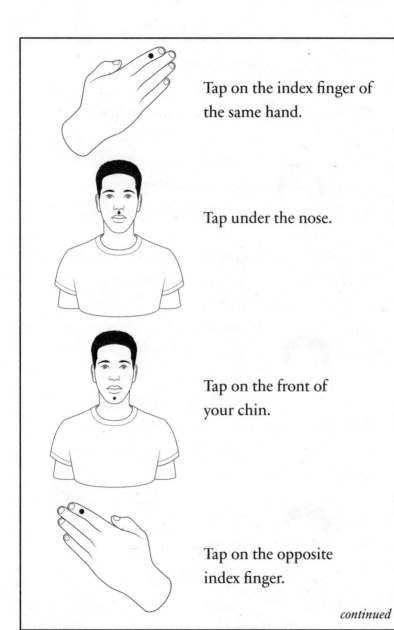

Tap on the index finger of the same hand.

Tap under the nose.

Tap on the front of your chin.

Tap on the opposite index finger.

continued

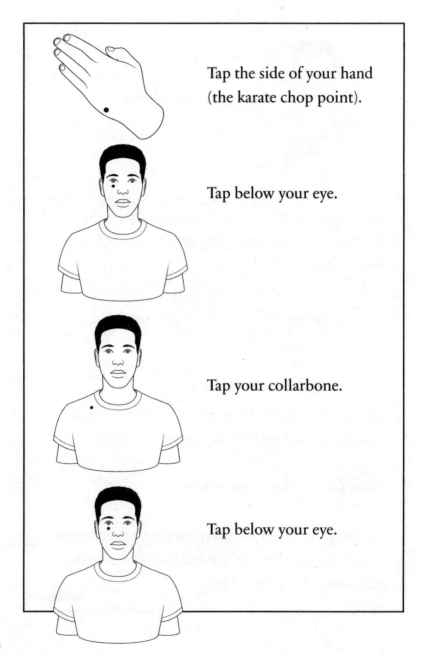

Tap the side of your hand (the karate chop point).

Tap below your eye.

Tap your collarbone.

Tap below your eye.

Tap your collarbone.

Place your hand in front of you and tap on the back of it between your ring finger and your little finger.

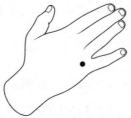

Continue to think about the unhappy feeling as you do this and each of the steps that follow:

Close your eyes and open them.

Keeping your head still, keep tapping between your ring finger and little finger and look down to the right, then down to the left.

continued

Keep tapping and rotate your eyes around 360 degrees clockwise, and now 360 degrees anti-clockwise (unless you suffer from motion sickness, in which case, skip this bit).

Now hum the first few lines of 'Happy Birthday' out loud.

Count out loud from one to five.

Once again hum the first few lines of 'Happy Birthday' out loud.

Stop and check – on a scale from one to 10, what number is the unhappy feeling at now?

If hardly any of the unwanted feelings are there, congratulations. If it has not reduced enough yet, just repeat the tapping sequence until it does.

You may want to take a break and then I am going to take you to another level with a super powerful technique.

The greatest therapeutic breakthrough in recent times

While I was in America, I also visited Dr Ronald Ruden – who is not only a Manhattan medical doctor but he also has a PhD in neuropharmacology. You are usually either a doctor in the trenches, or holed up knee-deep in research in a lab – but he's both. It was a beautiful day, so we went for a walk down Seventh Avenue. During our stroll I said: "Do you know, I read the wackiest book on the plane here, where this guy, Dr Callahan, who is a respectable academic, university professor and psychologist, has created a system where you tap on acupuncture and meridian points on the body to heal trauma and treat compulsion and anxiety. I've tested it on a couple of people and it actually worked." Ron was immediately interested so I gave him my copy of the book.

A few days later, I got an email from him saying: "I've tried this on a number of my patients including those with anxiety disorders and none of them took more than 15 minutes to cure. I'm going to research this whole area of psychosensory techniques." I didn't think any more of it at the time.

Over the following months, I learned as much as I could about it. From time to time, I also got emails from Dr Ruden about his scientific research. A year or so later, he rang me and explained that he'd created a completely new psycho-sensory therapy. It's totally different to TFT (which as you know, involves tapping on meridian points), but it does utilise touch in that it involves stroking the face, the sides of your arms, as well as visualisations to help people emotionally heal. He called it 'Havening', as in 'a safe haven'.

Some months later, I went through a relationship break-up and was in terrible emotional pain. It allowed me to discover first-hand the power of Havening. When you think about something upsetting, a picture, sound or both come to mind. For me, at the time, a vivid image of my now ex-girlfriend's face would be in full colour in my mind's eye as I experienced feelings of loss, betrayal and upset.

The next time I met Ron for dinner, he asked me how I was doing. When I said, "Badly," he said, "Slide your chair over here – I can help you." He began by stroking the sides of my arms, whilst I imagined walking on a beach, and he ran me through the Havening process. In less than 15 minutes, all of that pent-up sadness and anger had gone. It was miraculous. The large colour picture I'd had in my mind of my ex-girlfriend shrank to the size of a postage stamp, was drained of all colour and it gave me the freedom of indifference. It's stayed like that for more than a decade. I could remember that the experience had been upsetting but I could no longer feel upset. The thought of the relationship had been *de-linked* from the feeling. I couldn't have cared less! I said: "This is absolutely extraordinary."

I went round to his apartment the following day at 9am to find out everything I could about it. He had a mountain of academic papers the size of several phone directories stacked on top of each other. He put on a pot of coffee and told me he was going to "force feed me the science of Havening" – and that's exactly what he did over the next eight hours. He had produced a 'Primer' or textbook which contained a huge amount of science revealing exactly how his method uses a process of gentle and soothing touch which can permanently eliminate chronic physical and emotional pain without drugs or surgery – in minutes. As soon as I'd finished reading his findings and the science behind it I told him: "This is truly ground-breaking and this is going to change countless people's lives."

Today, Havening is the grand daddy of all of the psycho-sensory techniques. Until you have seen its almost miraculous power for emotional healing, as I have over the past decade, it's hard to believe it's real. I have included a Havening exercise in several of my books because it is such a quick and powerful way to heal our inner wounds. Now I'm going to explain and then guide you through a new, upgraded version, created by Dr Ruden, that works even *better* than before.

Patterns of repeated touch to parts of the body combined with visualisations can have a rapid, reliable and predictable effect on our feelings. The patterns of touch used in Havening are what enable a mother to comfort her baby and they are hard-wired into all of us. Havening combines these deep-rooted patterns of reassurance with sequences to break down the associations that trigger unhappy or uncomfortable feelings. As a result, in a matter of minutes, we can now reduce the intensity of an emotion or feeling of unhappiness and establish calm.

In addition, certain brain waves are associated with different functions in our lives. Beta waves are associated with being alert and anxious. Alpha waves represent a state of relaxed alertness. One wave is synonymous with really deep relaxation – the holy grail that we are all after in terms of therapy and healing – and that is Delta Waves. You get Delta Waves when you are deeply asleep, deeply relaxed or when you are doing Havening. Delta waves help to reconfigure traumatic or upsetting feelings. So, when you think about that upsetting thing, and then follow the Havening sequence, you flood your brain with Delta Waves and that creates a reverse effect biologically on the brain.

In the past Havening had eye movements as part of its process. But Dr Ruden's upgraded Havening protocol abandons this and instead you touch your forehead and the side of your cheeks – a bit like washing your face – as there is an abundance of key sensory receptors there. He has discovered this new pattern of touch dramatically increases the impact of the Havening process.

The second reason for the change in the Havening protocol is that some people confused it with EMDR (eye movement desensitisation and reprocessing) – a therapy that I feel has limitations. I've helped countless people who have tried EMDR before meeting me who found it worked for them temporarily but the results didn't last. Havening actually alters the landscape of your brain and so the results are almost always instantaneous, but crucially they tend to last.

Recently pop star Justin Bieber's therapist Dr Buzz Mingin revealed that he had used Havening with Justin to relieve his anxiety.

There is also hard science and a global movement that proves its benefits. I was involved in a pioneering scientific study at King's College, London, with military personnel who suffered from PTSD. Most had tried all sorts of other treatments but they hadn't worked. Havening was so successful in easing their trauma we widened it to victims of rape and people who were bereaved.

This book and system is not about treating extreme disorders like PTSD, that's for one-to-one therapy, but, along with the audio techniques, it will certainly help give you freedom from anxiety.

How trauma is encoded

When people go through a traumatic experience, a part of their consciousness stays stuck in the past, as part of their protection mechanism. Some people are able to code it so that while it was a really terrible thing and they can remember it happened, they don't feel upset by it. That's a functional way of processing it.

A dysfunctional way of thinking is when every day a part of you is thinking about that terrible thing that happened and can't seem to get over it. This is because there has been a physical change and a new neural pathway has been created in the brain that can immediately snap us back to that event.

More often than not, the mind also remembers it in a way that is very real, recreating feelings of anxiety, stress, fear, panic, anger or a mix of all of those feelings. This can have life altering consequences. The sad reality is that I regularly meet people who have experienced a trauma and for *years* have been reliving the stress and anxiety associated with that experience, over and over again. I sometimes ask: "How often do you think about that thing that happened

20 years ago that was awful but is in your past?" It can be as much as every hour of every day.

Today, despite decades of doctors and scientists studying the workings of the human brain, much of it is still not understood. However, we do know quite a bit about what happens to the brain after a traumatic event.

Sensory input is fed to our amygdala (the threat detector) along with data from the cortex (involved in thinking, learning, reasoning, emotions, consciousness and problem-solving) and through a series of complex responses meaning is ascribed to the event. So, for instance that could be that all dogs can bite, or all elevators are scary. If the trauma is seen as inescapable and has an emotional intensity, that causes a biological change in the brain – but the amazing thing is that the Havening technique easily reverses this process.

That's why at the end of a Havening session when I say to somebody: "Can you remember the upset?" They will say: "No! I can remember the event and it was bad, but I can't get the feelings back." That's because we have de-linked the thought from the feeling. So, you can have the thought about the upsetting thing that happened, but you can't feel the emotion, as the two are no longer connected.

During the pandemic, I've used this amazing technique at the sharp end as a tool for doctors, nurses and technicians. I met with a group of young, dynamic NHS trainee doctors and I did Havening with them. At first, they were completely sceptical – they didn't believe a word of it. However, the convincer for them was when they could think about something that was traumatic or upsetting and within a few minutes, they could no longer get upset about it.

One of the first people I helped using Havening was an extraordinary lady, Nicki Senior, who came to see me after she had suffered an ectopic pregnancy that almost cost her own life and left her deeply traumatised. I did Havening with her for trauma, grief and negative emotions in front of a small group of medical professionals. They were astonished and almost in disbelief that it worked so fast – literally in minutes. She told me: "Going from being trapped in a cycle of fear and negative feelings, to complete freedom from pain in a literal heartbeat will stay with me forever." Nicki and Dave went on to have a rainbow baby called Sebastian. She wanted to share her story in this book so others can understand Havening's extraordinary healing power.

I also used Havening to help a wonderful paramedic, Ross Smith, who was a broken man due to PTSD. His marriage

THE HAVENING TECHNIQUE

🔊 *You can download this audio technique now.*

Please read through the following exercise before you do it.

You should practise this sequence of eye movements, body touches and visualisations several times until you know it off by heart. Then you will be able to use it anytime you need to get rid of unhappy feelings and swiftly feel calm and relaxed.

1   Pay attention to any stress or traumatic memory you wish to re-code and notice what it looks like in your imagination and how stressful it feels. Now, rate its strength on a scale of one to 10, where 10 is the most powerful and one is the least. This is important as it lets you measure how much you are reducing it.

continued

2   Now, clear your mind, or just think about or imagine something nice.

3   Now, stroke your forehead and the cheeks of your face repeatedly.

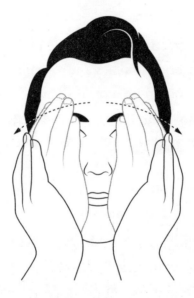

4   Now, stroke your hands down the sides of your arms from the top of your shoulders down to your elbows, and keep doing this downward stroking motion, again and again, throughout this process.

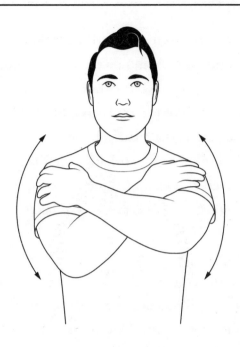

5   As you carry on stroking the sides of your arms, imagine you are walking on a beautiful beach. With each footstep you take in the sand, count out loud from one to 20.

6   Still stroking the sides of your arms, imagine you are walking outside in a beautiful garden. With each footstep you take in the grass, count out loud from one to 20.

continued

7   Now, open your eyes and check how you feel on your scale from one to 10. How much lower is the stress level now? If it is way down the bottom of the scale, congratulations – you have personally changed your own state. If you think that the unhappy feeling is not yet reduced enough, just repeat the Havening sequence until it is reduced as far as you want.

Many people experience remarkable positive changes immediately after a Havening session. However, even if you are one of those people, I recommend you do this Havening exercise as often as you want.

Now, let's build upon the calm you've just created with the next technique.

Reset your emotional equilibrium

Once you have learned Havening off by heart, I'd like you to use this incredible technique straight afterwards, which is like putting the icing on the cake. Inspired by Zen Master Genpo Roshi this is a way to recalibrate emotions. Using Havening and then Apex back-to-back resets your emotional ecosystem once you have reduced your anxiety.

I use my NLP version of The Apex Technique to counteract all sorts of uncomfortable feelings including stress, anger, guilt, grief and frustration. It is based on a technique from Neuro-Linguistic Programming known as 'Collapsed Anchors' as when two opposing emotions are experienced at the same time they rebalance.

This process gets you to summon an uncomfortable emotion then counter it with its opposite emotion. You then move your attention above your head, which has the effect of distancing yourself from the feelings. This begins the reset. It's a bit like a graphic equalizer that sounds shrill as only the treble is turned up. When you turn up the base, one balances the other out.

I often use it with 'chocaholics'. I ask them to think about eating a bar of their favourite sweet and initially they say: "Yum." Then I ask them to think about a taste and texture they are revolted by, such as broccoli or sardines. I then get them to imagine biting into the chocolate and tasting sardines, which triggers revulsion. So when desire and disgust are experienced at the same time one cancels out the other. The effect is not that they hate chocolate, but from that point forward they can take it or leave it, because they've reset their level of desire for it.

The second key to The Apex Technique's effectiveness is that by putting your attention above your head you are not *inside* the intensity of the emotion but you are *outside* of it – detached from the uncomfortable feeling.

THE APEX TECHNIQUE

🔊 *You can download this audio technique now.*

Read the exercise all the way through so that you understand it before starting.

1 Place your hands out in front of you with your palms turned up.

2 Next, let yourself focus on the feeling that is bothering you, whatever it is. It could be a fear, anger, or something else.

3 As you notice it, ask if there is anything that feeling would wish to say to you. If there is, make a note of it – if there is not, that is absolutely fine, too.

4 Now imagine holding the feeling in your left hand, in front of you and get in touch with it.

5 Now I'd like you to think of the opposite of that feeling – for example, peace, calm, comfort.

continued

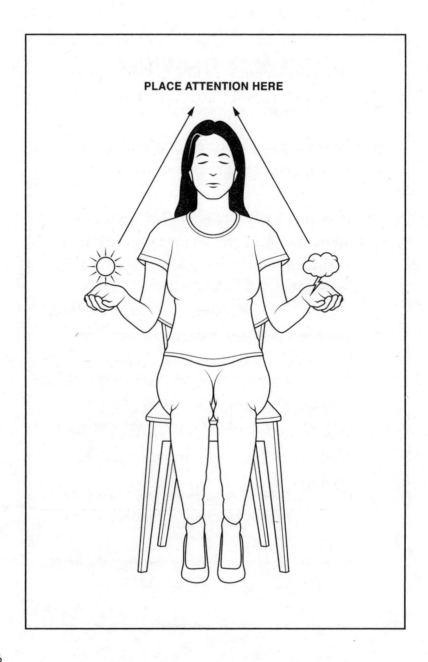

6 Bring that opposite feeling to mind – peace, calm, and comfort – and notice how it feels.

7 Now imagine placing that opposite, positive feeling in your right hand, in front of you.

8 Now move your attention up to a few inches above your head and keeping your attention in that position now experience both feelings at the same time.

9 Continue to feel the two emotions simultaneously with your attention above your head. As you do that, your emotional system will re-calibrate so that you can experience that difficult emotion at a lower level as it re-integrates into your emotional intelligence.

Using NLP for instant relief from anxiety

While most of the previous techniques are from the psycho-sensory field, I want to share with you one more, from the world of NLP that creates immediate relief from anxiety.

The word 'genius' is overused these days, but I feel fortunate to have met a number over the years from the fields of art, science, business and sport. Dr Richard Bandler is one of my favourite geniuses and, in my opinion, the most creative psychological mind of all time. NLP is the name he has given to his life's work and it is a psychological and behavioural technology that has significantly changed the world for the better.

Part of Richard's genius is that he observes things that other people miss. For example, he once explained to me that all feelings start somewhere in our bodies and then move somewhere else. When people are talking about fear, you often hear people say things like; "I have a feeling in the pit of my stomach." That is because for nearly everyone, fear starts in the bottom of the stomach and moves upwards.

So, I'd like you to try this experiment. Think about something scary and notice where the feeling starts. It will almost certainly start at the bottom of your stomach and move up to your chest!

The amazing news is that through visualisation you can get the feeling to go in the opposite direction, reduce it and then switch it off.

After I'd learned this technique from Richard, a few days later, I was on a helicopter flight in the South of France. I am not a nervous flyer at all – in fact, I absolutely love flying. However, as we approached the landing site, because there was another helicopter still on the pad below, we had to hold our position at 1,000 feet in the same spot. It was incredibly windy and we were bumping around a lot. I suddenly got a burst of fear – as did everyone else on board.

But then I remembered the spinning technique I had learned a few days before and decided to try it in that moment. I noticed the feeling was starting in the bottom of my stomach and moving up to my chest – and because the feeling is continually firing off, it's best to imagine it spinning like a wheel. I gave it a colour and imagined taking this spinning wheel out and seeing it in front of me. Then, I imagined flipping it over, so it was spinning in the opposite direction. I changed its colour and then imagined pulling the wheel into myself, so now it was moving down from my chest into the pit of my stomach. I kept it spinning faster and faster and like magic, the fear completely disappeared.

So now let me walk you through the technique…

THE SPINNING TECHNIQUE

🔊 *You can download this audio technique now.*

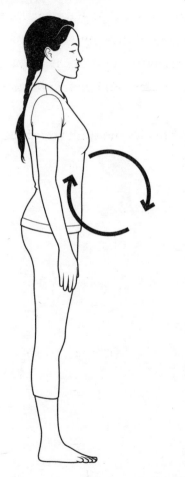

1   Think of something that really scares you and notice where the feeling of fear starts and moves to.

2   Give it a colour.

3   See it as a wheel spinning.

continued

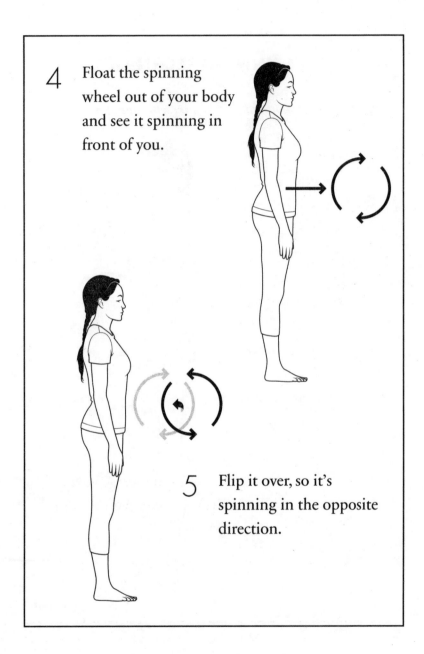

4 Float the spinning wheel out of your body and see it spinning in front of you.

5 Flip it over, so it's spinning in the opposite direction.

6   Change the colour.

7   Pull the new spinning
wheel back into
yourself and feel
it spinning in the
opposite direction.

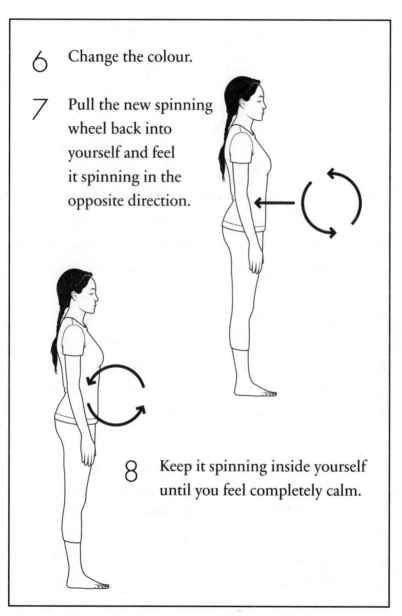

8   Keep it spinning inside yourself
until you feel completely calm.

Used with the written permission of Dr Richard Bandler.

The six-step reframe

For the final part of this section I am going to explain to you a powerful part of the hypnotic trance in the audio that comes with this system. It contains a technique from the world of NLP called The Six-Step Reframe. It is one of the greatest NLP techniques ever devised. You can use it to talk directly with someone's unconscious using hypnosis in what is known as a 'parts negotiation'. This technique is also super effective for people who suffer from panic attacks.

Panic attacks can often affect people who have had a significant change in their lives. Over the years I have worked with lots of young pop stars and actors who suddenly became very famous and when all the boundaries of their normal life changed, it triggered anxiety and panic attacks. People who have faced challenges in their work or private life can also start to have them.

A key part of a panic attack is the fear of fear itself. For those people, part of the fear is that the last time it happened it was terrible and they are frightened it's going to happen again and they won't have any warning. To the sufferer the panic attacks may seem random, which causes even more panic. They're constantly worried about when the next attack may occur, which leaves them in a state of constant anxiety. But panic attacks can be conquered.

When I am treating someone, I ask to talk to the part that's in charge of the panic attacks. I acknowledge that it has a function, which is protection, but there are other ways it can do that job without having to overprotect in future.

What's amazing about this is the unconscious mind then thinks to itself: "I can be on guard without having to be rolling with white knuckles at 'DEFCON 1.' It's only if I see something where I need to activate my internal defences, that I will go into high alert and fight or flight. But apart from that I can be relaxed."

It doesn't matter whether someone's panic attacks happen randomly, or if there is a trigger, this technique still works. The person doesn't have to even think about it, as it is all done at the unconscious level. I never cease to be amazed at its power.

And this technique is included in the hypnotic trance that comes with the audio downloads, so if you suffer from panic attacks use the hypnotic trance to help you overcome them.

You should now be feeling significantly calmer with more emotional equilibrium when you think about things that were challenging.

Practise these techniques as often as you feel you need to, until they become second nature.

Now that we've reduced the stress, it's time to boost good feelings!

Section Two

Deeper Calm, Building Resilience & Boosting Good Feelings

Now we've reduced the bad stuff, we are going to amplify the good stuff in your mind. Because you have so much more bandwidth, now it's not all being taken up by anxiety, this section is all about empowering you to start visualising happiness, success and tap into great 'states' of mind and body so you can feel great!

One of the questions I am often asked is: "What's the single most important thing that you have learned from all of your work with people?" The answer is:

You get more of what you focus on.

People often tell me, "I don't want to be stressed, I don't want to be anxious, I don't want to be frightened." They worry about worrying. In other words, they are focusing on what it is they DON'T want so they tend to get more of it. In this section, we're going to train your brain to focus on the good stuff you DO want – including positivity, creativity and bliss.

The facts about anxiety

There are a few simple things that you need to know about anxiety.

There are only two ways to feel good or bad – the first way is to <u>remember</u> something good or bad that <u>*happened*</u>. The second is to <u>imagine</u> something good or bad that <u>*could happen*</u>.

For example, if you start to even *think* about things that make you anxious, you change your body/brain chemistry and electricity in the same way as if you remember an event that *actually* took place.

What you practise, you get good at...

People that are anxious have practised making pictures and sounds in their minds that stress and frighten them. They've done it over-and-over again, and built up neural networks in their brains that mean they can do it very well. They've made anxiety a habit. Robert M. Sapolsky, a professor of biology and neurology says in his book *Why Zebras Don't Get Ulcers*: "Essentially, we humans live well enough and long enough, and are smart enough, to generate all sorts of stressful events purely in our heads." He adds: "We can experience wildly strong emotions (provoking our bodies into an accompanying uproar) linked to mere thoughts." This book and the audio techniques that go with it will help you make *calmness* a habit instead, which will make your life infinitely better.

I used to wonder why some people are stressed out while others don't seem to care about anything. My conclusion is that both these types of people are extremists. Constant anxiety is draining and the belief it keeps you safe is a fallacy as over-surviving all day and experiencing emergencies that never happen is exhausting and stops you thinking with clarity. However, those who never worry about anything also don't see or pay attention to potential dangers, and so they put themselves at risk too.

Of course, there are a few lucky people whose natural default is that they don't get really upset about things but they still keep alert enough to spot trouble on the horizon and deal with it. Back in the '80s, one of the pilots who taught me to fly was like that. Once, we were coming in to land in a Cessna and I forgot to put the flaps down, which was a really dangerous thing to do. As I continued my descent, he calmly said, "We are going to die." I screamed, "Argh! Flaps!" and disaster was averted. Afterwards, I asked him, "What would have happened if I hadn't remembered?" He laughed, "I would have done it, of course, but I just thought you should know, as you will be flying on your own in a week or two."

I have spent decades studying a wide range of individuals and what makes some people more anxious than others as well as more successful. I have found the highest achievers systematically evaluate risk and potential outcomes before making decisions until it becomes second nature. As a result, these people are functional, successful and happy. So my objective is not just to make you free from anxiety, but also help you become happier and even more functional.

The next fundamental fact about anxiety is:

You have a CHOICE in how you deal with anxiety.

Dr Hans Selye, who is known as 'the father of stress research' once said, "It's not stress that kills us, it is our reaction to it." That's why you don't have to change your external circumstances to overcome anxiety, like your job or your relationship – it's about working on *yourself*. I have met countless people that have been anxious for years, yet suddenly in the space of minutes, hours or days after using these techniques, their whole perspective changes. Key to that is realising you are not a powerless victim of your anxiety. Dr Selye was also explicit about this, saying, "Adopting the right attitude can convert a negative stress into a positive one."

The argument about nature/nurture and environment/ genetics is on-going and will almost certainly continue, but I believe that some people have 'inherited' anxiety from one of their parents. We can pick up behaviours from those people around us who are influential characters, early in our lives.

In addition, words said at a moment of emotional intensity by somebody in authority, have the power of a hypnotic suggestion. One of the reasons public speaking is such a prevalent phobia in the western world is because, as a child, we get to stand up in front of the class, read out loud, somebody points out all of the mistakes and other people snigger. But the good news is because it is a *learned* behaviour it can also be *unlearned*.

The importance of your state of being

Everything you do, from boiling an egg to running a business is driven by your 'behaviours'. Your behaviours are, in turn, driven by your state of mind and body. Examples of states are things like confidence, love, apathy, fear, creativity and happiness. Anxiety is a state, too. There are three things that create our 'state' of being. They are:

- The internal dialogue in our head.
- The internal pictures or movies we make in our mind.
- Our physiology.

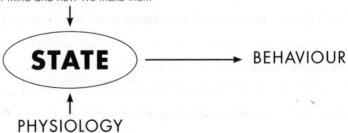

INTERNAL
REPRESENTATIONS
The pictures and sounds we make in
our mind and how we make them

STATE ⟶ BEHAVIOUR

PHYSIOLOGY
Posture, muscular tension, breathing, etc

The state of mind that you are in when you are sitting at the computer is different to when you are relaxing in a bath. Your state of mind when you are giving a presentation is different to when you are having a drink down the pub with your friends, or driving a car. All day long you are shifting from one state to another. But if you are experiencing too much anxiety you are on guard, preparing for emergencies that don't happen, your brain and body chemistry is changing and tensing up and it ends up becoming a self-reinforcing loop that preoccupies you.

I have dyslexia and so when I look at words I can't see if the letters are in the right order – it just doesn't compute somehow. In the old-fashioned education system you were thought to be and told you were stupid because you couldn't spell properly. One of my school reports actually said I would never amount to anything. Fifty years ago you could say that sort of thing. Now it would be considered child abuse. Some people would have felt crushed by that, but I made a choice, and my choice was "I'll show you!"

That said, early in my career I believe there was some impact as I suffered from 'Imposter Syndrome' and I know I am not alone in having those feelings. I realised this when a friend of mine introduced me to Dennis Selinger who was a super-agent that represented Michael Caine, Roger Moore, Sean Connery and Peter Sellers amongst many other stars and he wanted to be my agent. I found it hard to accept that someone of his amazing status was interested in me. My inner voice would go, "I can't believe he wants to represent you – what have you possibly got to offer compared to all these others stars?" A lot of the time I was operating out of stress, a fear of not being good enough, not delivering, of being found out.

Many people recognise the feeling when the perfectionist in us says, "They are going to find out I'm really not that good at all." Even after you have succeeded at something, you can still talk yourself out of acknowledging your achievement. Perfectionists also constantly question what they do. I was very much like that. I was frightened I wasn't good enough, that my performances wouldn't be right and even if they did work out, I'd think, "Well, I got away with it this time." I was constantly beating myself up. I lived in this world of sometimes moving towards success, but a lot of the time I was driven by the fear of failure. It was completely exhausting. I nearly ended up mentally and physically burned out.

Everything changed for me when I learned the techniques in this section, which are essentially simple hypnotic exercises and NLP. First, I learned to monitor my internal dialogue. I realised the internal voice in my mind talked incessantly at a hundred miles an hour, was abrupt, harsh, at times sarcastic. I had been a slightly nervous, nerdy kid and I wasn't a natural stage performer as I'd been a radio DJ who sat in a box and talked into a microphone and at times, my internal critic undermined my confidence.

Then I noticed I was continually making pictures in my mind of things going wrong, which was fair enough, as I was alerting myself to potential problems, but I wasn't making enough pictures or movies of myself doing things *right*! In the '20s Alfred Adler developed a therapeutic technique that he called 'Acting As If' which is about manifesting what you want. It enabled people to practise positive behaviours instead of being entrenched in negative ones. I like to think of it more in terms of The Law of Attraction; that positive or negative thoughts can beget positive or negative experiences. So the final piece of the jigsaw was when I changed my physiology and realised when I felt anxious, I tensed up and looked down a lot; making myself look smaller than I actually was. So I changed it. I would hold my head up high, relax my shoulders and I would imagine stepping into a more confident me before I would walk on stage or go into a meeting.

Once I combined all three (my new encouraging internal dialogue, the success movies, and my confident body posture), I became a different person. Instead of being overwhelmed and daunted, my fledgling career as a stage hypnotist became exciting and an opportunity. People started saying, "There's something different about you. You seem much more at ease with yourself, what's going on?" I said, "I'm doing these new techniques I've learned." I discovered an infinitely more enjoyable mind-set to live in which then opened up my world and eventually led me to the career and life I have today. My personal experience means I firmly believe that it isn't what you are born with or what happens to you that shapes your destiny. It's the *choices* you make.

I recently did one of my Positivity Podcasts with Oscar-nominated, Emmy award-winning writer, director and radio producer Armando Iannucci who offered an amazing insight into how he conquered the Imposter Syndrome mind-set too. Early in his career he felt "any day now I'm going to be found out". Even when he started a new project he'd often think: "This is going to be terrible, this is going to be the worst thing ever." He said a revelation for him was the realisation that, "Hang on, everyone is thinking the same!" That got him through that barrier of thinking. He put his head down and *went for it* instead of tying himself in knots. His main piece of advice to people is to ask themselves when they are in this mind-set: "What's the worst that could happen?"

What's important to take from this is that everyone feels nervous when they are stepping out of their comfort zone. But when you realise (within the boundaries of reason) that you are not bound by your perceived limitations and fears – as they are just ideas you have picked up along the way – the parameters of what could be possible are widened.

And remember NOBODY is perfect – in fact, it's our imperfections that make us human. If you took an orchestra full of robots and put them in the Albert Hall to play a symphony they would perform it absolutely perfectly. There wouldn't be a note wrong. However, it wouldn't have soul, as it's the imperfection that gives it its humanity. The moral of this is, do you want to be like a robot or do you want to be someone who through imperfection is human, rather than just a machine?

The internal dialogue in our mind

It's really important to make friends with your internal dialogue, stop your unnecessary inner 'negative talk' and get your inner voice to be encouraging, which will start to increase good feelings. I want to introduce you to a stunningly simple technique that can instantly stop your inner voice sabotaging you, telling you there are threats everywhere or that everything is 'the end of the world.'

Everybody uses an inner voice all day long to guide them through life. Without even thinking, you'll say in your mind, "Oh, I must remember to call this person" or "They look nice" or "What if I do it like this?" The problem arises when a negative internal voice runs an endless commentary that holds us back, limits our potential and makes us feel unnecessarily bad. If you make a mistake, you are likely to be very harsh on yourself, calling yourself 'an idiot!' or even worse. When you look in the mirror in the morning, you may be super critical and shred your own confidence before you even walk out of the door. Usually, when people are anxious, their internal dialogue is often fast. It is shrill, worried, concerned and has an intensity and urgency about it. When you begin to take control of your inner voice, you can turn down the volume on the bad stuff and amplify the good.

A few years back I worked with a very famous actress who had stage fright. I said to her: "Who is the person you most admire who never gets nervous?" She said, "The legendary Sir Ian McKellen. Even if something goes horribly wrong, he's unflappable." A few months later, I ended up sitting next to him at a dinner function. I said, "Sir Ian, is it really true you never get stage fright?" He said, "It's true." So, I asked him, "How do you do it?" He told me when he first started out as a very young actor in repertory theatre he popped into a cafe across the road following a matinee performance. Two people sat behind him, not realising it was him, and gossiped about how rubbish they thought he was. He told me he took that negative feedback with him on stage that night and his performance suffered as he was remembering that negative critique. Then he told me, "I never took it on the stage with me ever again." He'd turned his unnecessary internal dialogue off. Some people can do this just instantaneously, and others have to practise before they get the hang of it.

Just by starting to pay attention to your inner voice, you begin to take back your power, so it's a really good idea to just notice what it's saying and the way it's saying it for the next few days objectively and see if it's helping you or not.

For some people, the act of tuning in is enough for you to go, "Hang on a minute, I'm winding myself up! I'm going to stop." Others find changing the location and tone of the voice inside your head or turning it down can reduce anxiety and increase confidence. This next technique will show you how.

CONTROLLING YOUR INTERNAL DIALOGUE

🔊 *You can download this audio technique now.*

1   Locate your inner voice. Ask yourself, "Where is my internal voice?" Notice the location where you hear the words coming from. Is it the front of your head, the back, or the side?

2   Now I want you to imagine how your inner voice sounds when it's anxious and where it's located – is it front, centre, back?

3   Now, talk to yourself in a calm, relaxed and gentle way. Is your inner voice louder or softer than usual? Is it clearer and easier to hear? Is it stronger or weaker? Do you speak faster or slower?

4   Now, put that voice in the same location as where your old internal voice was located.

continued

5   Now, in a strong, calm voice, say these words in your mind, over and over again, "All is well... All is well..." Continue for as long as you need to. Notice how that makes you *feel*.

6   Next, think of something that makes you anxious and of some of the things you have told yourself in the past like, "I'm rubbish at giving presentations" or "I've never been good at that".

7   For each statement, come up with its positive opposite e.g., "I'm great at giving presentations" or "I'm really good at that".

8   Repeat the new, positive affirmations to yourself in your new, calm voice inside your mind. Say them over and over again.

Once you've got the hang of that, it's time to build on this technique and train your internal dialogue to be more confident with the following technique.

The inner critic

The next technique will cause that unnecessarily critical inner voice of gloom, doom, stress, worry and fear to lose its power over you. Someone asked me the other day: "If you read or hear something negative about you, how do you not let it bug you all day?" The answer is simple. I recall the words but in the voice of Mickey Mouse, so I just can't take it seriously. At one of my recent events, a lady told me a heart-breaking story that had scarred her for 50 years. She said, "My mother said to me: 'I wish you'd never been born, you ruined my life.'"

Remember, when something negative is said at a moment of emotional intensity by somebody in authority, it has the power of a hypnotic suggestion. So it had had a profound effect on her. But I was able to negate those words in minutes. I told her, "I want you to remember your mother saying it, but make her voice sound like Mickey Mouse's high-pitched voice." Her tears and the pain that she had carried for half a century dissipated. She was able to suddenly let it go and burst into laughter!

I recently did a seminar where I practised this with a lady who found she couldn't turn her internal negative voice off but when we turned the volume down and then turned it into Mickey Mouse she said: "Oh I can't take it seriously anymore". So, if you are constantly saying to yourself, "I'm an anxious person" or "The world is going to end" or "It's all going to go horribly wrong" and "Life is terrible!", repeat it in a Mickey Mouse voice inside your mind. By making scary or upsetting things sound ridiculous, it strips them of their power.

CONTROLLING THE INNER CRITIC

◀)) *You can download this audio technique now.*

1   Think about a time when you criticised yourself severely and remember what you said.

2   Listen carefully to your inner voice and where it is. Is it in the front or back of your head? Somewhere else? Notice where it is coming from, what tone it has and how loud it is.

3   Now, change the sound of the internal voice
     so it sounds like Mickey Mouse or a crazy
     cartoon character.

4   Next, hold your hand up in front of you with
     the thumb pointing upwards and imagine
     floating that voice away from your head and
     out to your thumb.

5   Now, imagine hearing that same critical voice
     again but with your voice coming from your
     thumb and speaking like Mickey Mouse.

6   Now, listen again, whilst feeling relaxed and
     amused by the silly tone of the voice you are
     hearing.

OK. Now, you are really getting control of your internal dialogue – let's take it to the next level.

Your internal dialogue

I'd now like to show you another super simple way to continue to reduce your anxiety and install calm, good feelings. It is something I'd like you to start each day with.

There is a body of work called *The Hidden Messages In Water* by Dr Masaru Emoto in which he claims that water can be affected by positive or negative words or emotions. Dr Emoto took pure, distilled water and exposed it to different stimuli – words, pictures, sounds, music and even prayer – then he froze it and photographed the ice crystals. The crystals in water exposed to loving words were beautiful and symmetrical while those subjected to hate became jangly, disfigured and distorted. While Dr Emoto's work has attracted controversy, it gives an insight into how things you say to yourself or out loud all day long can impact you, not only emotionally but potentially even at a molecular level as 75 per cent of all biological tissue is water.

Dr Ruden and I used this affirmation through the pandemic for emergency workers at the end of their shift. It touches on an emerging area of psycho-neuro-immunology (PNI)

– looking at how psychology and neurology affects our health. So it shouldn't just make you feel good, it should improve your wellbeing too.

CALMING YOUR INTERNAL DIALOGUE

🔊 *You can download this audio technique now.*

1   Get quiet and still.

2   In a gentle, powerful voice inside your mind now say these words over and over:

Safe. Peaceful. Hopeful. Calm. All is well.

3   Notice how you feel.

Now we've worked on your internal dialogue, let's move on to the next stage.

The movies of the mind

The second thing that influences our 'state' of being is the *pictures or movies we make in our mind*. So the next step of building a happier, calmer life is to take control of our imagination, which is normally great at dreaming up all of the scenarios that could go wrong – and rewrite the script into a movie where everything goes right! Dr Richard Bandler says, "Disappointment requires adequate planning." By thinking about all the worst-case scenarios and nothing else, it has a greater potential to become a self-fulfilling prophecy.

The good news is, because the human nervous system doesn't recognise the difference between a real and a vividly imagined experience, we are going to visualise feeling good, optimistic, successful and joyous and the effect will be the same as if it has actually happened for real. When I get a feeling of foreboding or anxiety, I stop and ask myself, "What am I anxious about?", "What is the picture, movie or the sound associated with it that comes to mind?" and I listen to it. I ask myself, "What can I do about this?" I take action, and then I play another movie in my mind imagining it going exactly the way that I'd like it to. I will even add in a few challenges and visualise myself overcoming them smoothly. And that's the difference that makes the difference! Of course, once again, you have to practise this process to get good at it.

Psychologists also refer to something they call 'background stress'. By that they don't mean the burst of adrenaline that comes if someone puts a gun to your head. Instead, it's lots of little bits of stress having a cumulative effect.

During the Covid-19 pandemic I noticed that some mornings I would have a feeling of foreboding, of anxiety. I couldn't put my finger on it. I said to my wife Kate: "I am anxious," and she said: "Yes, so am I." One day, I watched the news continuously and I found myself catastrophising: "What if my family gets sick? What if I get sick? What about the economy? What's going to happen to the world?" My mind had automatically begun playing worst-case scenarios over and over again. So, I stopped. I gave myself the space to acknowledge those feelings and asked myself why I was having them. I realised, the world was such a different, uncertain place, the news was full of scary stories about the virus and it was literally playing on my mind. What I learned from that experience was that if I spent all day watching worst-case scenario news on a loop, I would upset myself so much that it triggered anxiety. I spoke to a lot of my friends on Skype and Zoom and they were experiencing the same thing.

I once worked with a mother who suddenly developed the habit of freaking out every few minutes of the day, imagining her baby had escaped out of the back gate or was drowning in her pool. Her natural, maternal mechanism was overdoing its job. I simply put her in a trance and asked her protection mechanism to do its job without over-signalling. The aim was to achieve a balance – just enough preparation and anxiety to head off problems at the pass, but not so much you get into over-thinking constantly.

Athletes run the opposite of disaster movies in their mind by doing something called 'mental rehearsal' before a race or a match where they imagine the event going really well and they do it over and over again. This affects their 'state' – it even affects their muscle memory and their performance and enables them to 'practise' being a winner so it's familiar to them by the time it gets to the real thing. I remember years ago talking to one of the most successful decathletes of all time, Daley Thompson, who became only the second competitor in history to win the decathlon at two Olympic games in 1980 and 1984 as well as being a four-time record breaker. Amazingly, he did not lose a decathlon for a staggering nine years. He told me, "I'm not really into this sports psychology, Paul. I don't think it's really for me". So I asked him, "Do you ever think about an event before you do it?" He replied, "Every single step. Over and over again."

Some people use my techniques, not because they are anxious, but in order to reach a peak state of performance. Two celebrities who have also publicly spoken about how I've helped them are The Who's Roger Daltrey who is a confident person, but before he goes on stage uses my confidence trance so he delivers at his absolute best. Roger *works* at feeling as good as he possibly can! While comedian Russell Brand, who is also brimming with confidence, wants to be in a state of total focus, and alert, yet calm, when he walks on stage – so he can give 1,000 per cent. For them, using these techniques is all about boosting good feelings.

A journalist who interviewed me recently, told me he'd read one of my early self-help books that had completely changed his life. There was a girl he really wanted to ask out but he was worried about being rejected. He explained that after reading my book, he changed his internal dialogue which made him more confident. I asked, "So, what happened?" He replied, "We've been married for 15 years."

Harnessing the power of the pictures and movies of your mind

When people are anxious, their brain is running them and they are not running their brain. The way you picture things in your mind can strip the potency of a negative emotion but also exponentially increase the feel-good power of a positive one.

When you remember things that feel great, it's a good idea to step *inside* the memory and become a part of the image or movie in your mind, like you're back there again now – this is something that is known as being *'associated'*.

But when you are remembering things that are uncomfortable, traumatic or unhappy, step *outside* of the memory – be someone on the *outside* looking in, like it's happening to somebody else. This is known as *'disassociated'*. Essentially you are telling yourself: 'Not that, but *this* instead.' By stepping into more and more good times you are stacking them one on top of another – building a new landscape of your life.

Being inside a memory intensifies the feeling.

**Being outside a memory reduces
the intensity of the feeling.**

I used this technique in the darkest time of my life when my father died in 2011 and I was overwhelmed by grief. We'd thought he was getting better and when he passed away suddenly and unexpectedly, it was like being hit by a freight train emotionally. Naively I thought, "I will be able to tough this out." But I became consumed by the loss. I went to that place where you can't see any point in anything, any future. Then, I had an epiphany. I realised I was remembering the last few months of his life in hospital, instead of the 84 fantastic years of him being my vibrant, loving father.

So, I did a simple process – every time I caught myself feeling bad and remembering that time back in the hospital, I stepped out of myself in that picture and floated back, like I was looking into a scene on a TV screen. I could see the back of my head. Then I drained the entire colour out of that image of the hospital room, made it black and white and shrunk it down to the size of a postage stamp. I then immediately brought in a big, vibrant, colour memory of a good time with my dad and I put myself inside that, reliving those beautiful moments again. I remembered when we played football together, when we sat and laughed at a film, when he was kind and supportive and when I felt loved. By doing this, I was saying to my brain, "Not that – but *this* instead." By installing the wonderful times over and over again, it meant within a day or two, my brain automatically went to good times instead of bad. I kept practising, and for me now, the default setting when I think of my dad is the happy times. I still miss him but I am no longer overwhelmed with his loss.

So, let's practise this now.

STEP INTO THE GOOD TIMES

🔊 *You can download this audio technique now.*

Remember a time when you felt good. Imagine watching a movie of it happening to you now.

continued

107

Return to it like you are back there again. See what you saw, hear what you heard and feel how you felt. When you do that, you will start to feel good, as you are inside the memory, you are inside the movie. That is called 'associated'.

Now make the colours richer, brighter and bolder and the sounds louder. Notice what happens to how you feel.

STEP OUT OF THE BAD TIMES

 *You can download this audio technique now.*

Now I'd like you to remember a time when you had a mildly upsetting experience – it could be an argument or a disappointment.

Now I want you to stop and freeze that image in your mind. Literally press the pause button.

Next, step out of the picture and float it further and further away from you, so you can see the back of your head in the image like it's happening to somebody else, over there.

Next, drain the colour out of the image, so it is black and white and shrink it down in size until it's as small as a postage stamp.

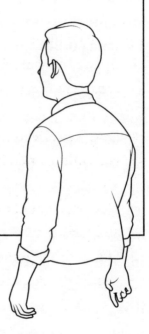

Creating new behaviours

The final step of harnessing the movies and pictures in your mind in order to boost good feelings is to visualise life going brilliantly.

Many people suffer from performance anxiety or presentation anxiety in things like giving a public talk, making presentations at work or even going on a date. Generally people who are nervous on a date have imagined 'being found out' or 'not being good enough'.

The way that people create their anxiety is by vividly imaging things going badly over and over again, so that when they actually get to give their presentation or go on their date they have already set themselves up for disaster. Once someone is gripped by self-doubt or worry it becomes a self-reinforcing loop.

A simple technique to overcome performance or presentation anxiety is to watch a movie in your imagination of things going well and then associate or step into yourself in the movie. It trains your brain to have the self-fulfilling prophecy of what you actually *want to have happen*.

So if you imagine giving a perfect presentation, you will perfect it and get it really good in your mind first and then you will step into it. Instead of imagining failing over and over again, you are setting yourself up for success.

THE NEW BEHAVIOUR GENERATOR

🔊 *You can download this audio technique now.*

1 Close your eyes and imagine you can see a cinema screen in front of you.

2 On the screen watch a movie of how you would ideally like to be and act in an upcoming event. Notice your posture, expression and manner. The way you interact with other people and the world. The light behind your eyes, the sound of your voice, everything that lets you know you are in a relaxed, alert state of total confidence, in the zone.

3   When the movie of you looks really good, float into the screen and into yourself.

4   See through the eyes of your more confident self, hear your internal dialogue, and feel how good it feels.

Do this process as often as you need to in order to train your brain for success.

Now, it's time to put the final bit of the jigsaw into place...

The power of physiology

By the time you have reached this point, you will have increased the feel-good emotions in your mind. Now it's time to address the third part of the equation of how we create our 'state', which is *physiology*.

Our posture, muscle tension and breathing all influence the way we feel. Anxious people are tense in their mind, leading them to be tense in their body, with physical symptoms including a tight jaw and tense shoulders.

When we relax our body, or if somebody relaxes it for us, say with a massage, they physically soften the muscles and then, in turn, the mind relaxes too. This comes back to the fact that the mind and body are in a loop, continuously influencing each other. So if you relax your mind using any of these techniques, your body will relax too.

When people with anxiety come to see me in my study you can see stress etched on their face. They often grip the chair with their hands, their breathing is often shallower and everything about them screams: "I'm tense!"

Once I have done the techniques to take their stress away they often look years younger. That's because the physical manifestation of their stress melts away too.

Years ago, when I was a stage performer, a friend of mine who is a masseuse came round to see me before the show and said, "Let me do a little massage on you." She got me really relaxed, but I discovered this was the opposite of what I needed! Normally I'll bounce out on stage, bursting with energy and say, "Good evening, ladies and gentlemen!" with high energy. I was so chilled out I didn't have that adrenaline burst before walking on stage that brings me to life!

I remember once reading an article about Bruce Springsteen where he'd been asked if he ever got nervous before he went on stage. Apparently, before performing in front of a huge audience, he gets a sensation in his stomach and that's when he knows he's ready to rock! I remember thinking, "This sounds like the early stages of fear!" but because it's not excessive, it remains in the category of excitement and enables him to perform at his peak.

Sir Roger Moore told me he learned the power of physiology when his first acting teacher asked him: "How tall are you?" and he replied, "6ft 2in." He asked him: "Why don't you stand like you are 6ft 2?" He changed his physiology and from that point his career started to take off!

So, take notice of your physiology – are you clenching your jaw, hunching your shoulders, or looking downwards a lot? If so, change it!

Your Ultradian Rhythm

Most people are aware of our Circadian Rhythm, which is our sleep and wake cycle. But there is also a second cycle called the *Ultradian Rhythm*, which is just as important.

The word 'Ultradian' means 'many times a day' and this is the key to it. It is a natural cycle of rest and alertness that occurs roughly every 90 minutes. Tapping into its natural rhythm can give you a healing, restorative break, which boosts physical, mental and emotional health.

Dr Ernest Rossi, a therapist and pioneer in mind and body healing discovered the power of the Ultradian Rhythm. He believed that the ebb and flow of consciousness is key to our wellbeing and if we override each 90-minute cycle instead of taking a break (often by knocking back a double espresso and concentrating even harder!) it puts our bodies under more and more stress which is bad for us.

One of the problems of modern life is that we don't recognise the value of our Ultradian Rhythm. For example, at school we are told, "Stop daydreaming!" Of course, there are times such as when you are driving or operating machinery when you need to override it, but if it's safe and appropriate to do so, once or twice a day, just go with it. You may find yourself daydreaming, your thoughts will slow down and you will feel a sweet, soft feeling in your muscles. As you relax into that, a mini trance-like state develops, you may even slide into a power nap. Just let your mind wander, and it will be like a battery recharge and a natural reset.

Lots of famous people throughout history have harnessed their Ultradian Rhythm. During World War Two, Prime Minister Winston Churchill swore by his afternoon power nap. He wrote in his memoirs, "Nature had not intended mankind to work from eight in the morning until midnight without the refreshment of blessed oblivion which, even if it only lasts 20 minutes, is sufficient to renew all the vital forces." He reportedly kept a bed in the Houses of Parliament to ensure he never missed one.

Albert Einstein, one of the most creative thinkers of all time, had a genius way of managing his breaks. He would hold a spoon in his hand and when he dropped it and it clunked as it hit the floor, he'd wake back up.

The artist Salvador Dali took micro-naps to refresh his mind and boost creativity. Similarly to Einstein, it is said that he would sit in a chair holding a big key pressed between his thumb and his forefinger, which would drop with a clang when he relaxed and wake him. He believed the short nap 'revivified' both his mind and body.

Celia Lacaux and Delphine Oudiette, sleep researchers at the Paris Brain Institute, were part of a team who asked 103 volunteers to complete a series of maths problems. They were asked to undertake a version of Dali's method, but by holding a plastic bottle in their fingertips, rather than a key. They discovered that those who took mini naps and who reached a sweet spot of sleep onset (where they were in the zone between being awake and asleep) were nearly *three times* more likely to solve maths problems than those who didn't. That 'in between' phase was like a creative trigger and led to Eureka moments!

A part of Walt Disney's creative process was daydreaming purposefully.

Tesla entrepreneur Elon Musk is known for being a daydreamer as a child, while the great Austrian composer Wolfgang Amadeus Mozart daydreamed about music.

If I am working, writing or teaching, I know that 90 minutes is the optimal amount of time before you get diminishing returns and so I will try to take a break.

Twice a day, I also allow myself to daydream. I find my 'sweet spot' in a number of ways. Sometimes I sit back and watch the sky, I'll watch a mindless TV show, do a meditation, or turn off the TV and sit with my eyes closed while calming down my system. Experiment with what works for you.

The three best self-hypnosis techniques

After all of the psycho-sensory and NLP techniques I have guided you through, it's now time to learn self-hypnosis. I am going to take you through this in stages. The first technique will teach you how to step into a state of calm meditation. Then, we will build on this by showing you how to connect with your internal world to deeply relax which will make you feel fantastic.

Like anything, the more you practise self-hypnosis, the better you get. Using meditation and trance can help you become the master of your own mind. Years ago, meditation seemed like some kind of new-age, weird pastime but now it is the norm for millions of people from all walks of life. One of the best technical definitions of a hypnotic state is Milton Erickson's, who described it as: "The loss of the multiplicity of the foci of attention." The mind we actively think with consciously holds only a handful of ideas at any one time. The larger mind is the unconscious mind, which means it's a great tool for solving problems and hypnosis can help us to tap into that.

Many people have the misconception that hypnosis is the same as sleep, but it's not. Sleep is where you are unconscious – you go through different stages and you dream. Hypnosis is more like a *daydream* for the majority of people. There are lots of different characteristics, but commonly people lose awareness of time, they stop focusing on things going on in the external world and they start focusing on things in their internal world. It can also help you profoundly relax. Over the years, some people have asked me, "What if I don't wake up?" Let me reassure you, *nobody* has ever failed to wake up from hypnosis! They may have been tired, so they drifted into sleep and then woke up, but nobody has failed to come out of trance.

My first experience of hypnosis was when I was working for local radio in the '80s. I was sent to interview the local hypnotist. I was in a state of massive upset as I'd just broken up with my girlfriend, the people in the flat where I was living were keeping me up at night and I was having a really bad day at work. All of that cumulative stress was getting on top of me. When I arrived, the hypnotist said: "Rather than me explaining it to you, let me hypnotise you to calm you down." I was sceptical but I said: "Go ahead, try your best." In just 30 minutes I became calm, I had a renewed clarity of mind and all my troubles seemed to melt away into the distance. He said: "You needed that didn't you?" and I replied: "Wow! I feel so much better!" That's what set me on the road to where I am today. As I've already mentioned I believe there are 'destiny moments' in people's lives and that was one of mine. I asked him: "Have you got a book on this?" and he gave me my first book on hypnosis. It all happened because I'd shown up to interview him, upset, anxious and wound up like you wouldn't believe which led me to discover first hand just how transformative hypnosis can be.

After my day job as a radio DJ, I started experimenting on everyone and anyone I knew in the evenings and weekends. At first, I'd be at a party and during the course of a chat I'd sometimes say: "I'm learning hypnosis" and when people said: "It won't work on me" I'd reply: "Shall we find out?" for fun. I went on to do the ITV show *The Hypnotic World Of Paul McKenna* and all the while I was exploring the powerful therapeutic side of hypnosis.

One of my friends wanted to quit smoking, so I decided: "Let's see if I can help you with that." By using hypnosis, it worked. Shortly after, a friend asked if I could help his son, who was not a model student by any stretch of the imagination, who was worried they wouldn't pass a biology exam and they needed some simple relaxation techniques. I had also just been reading everything that happens to us is stored as a multi-sensory recording in the unconscious mind. So I asked him: "Were you in the lessons?" When he said: "Yes," I thought: "This could work!" I gently put him into a simple meditative trance, saying: "Relax... close your eyes..." and I gave him a simple suggestion of: "You will remember everything from the classes you attended that you need relating to the exam tomorrow and you will feel relaxed." He passed with flying colours as he wasn't stressed out with all the pressure. It became clear to me that hypnosis could change people's lives and I decided to focus on that.

Today, if I have a creative problem, I will do self-hypnosis. Some people do a form of it by going to bed and asking themselves about a problem before 'sleeping on it', and sometimes they have a solution in the morning, but you can also do it with self-hypnosis over a shorter time. Sometimes, I go into big corporations and I do 'strategic planning' where people close their eyes, they relax, go off into the future and imagine what their product or service is like, what their competitors are up to, how the world is, etc. – even this is a form of it.

I also use hypnosis as a tool to address fear, anxiety and phobias. When I cure a person of a flying phobia, not only do I reduce their feelings of fear, I then put confidence, bliss and a bit of excitement in their mind about where they are going. Occasionally, I hypnotise someone so they can sleep on a plane, which is the absolute antithesis of anxiety, and, in my mind, a job well done.

When I do seminars on hypnosis, and help people tap into their inner calm, there is always a side effect that never ceases to amaze me. By the second day many people look younger because the stress that has been etched over their faces melts away. It's because they have been going in and out of trance and deeply relaxing, so it's like they have been away on a fabulous holiday.

Simple self-hypnosis

Let's start with the simplest self-hypnosis technique, which is Systematic Relaxation, as it's easy to learn yet it's super effective. People sometimes ask me, "What is the difference between meditation and hypnosis?" The main one is that with hypnosis you usually have a *specific intent*. The intent with this is to install a deep sense of relaxation in the body and mind – and for that reason it's commonly used at the end of a yoga session. Once you are comfortable with it and have practised it several times you can do it instantly.

The five primary stages of self-hypnosis are:

1   Make yourself comfortable (remove contact lenses, loosen your collar/belt, go to the toilet, etc.).

2   Set the intent or purpose for the trance – e.g. relaxation, energy regeneration, problem solving.

3   Set a time limit for your trance and ensure that you will not be disturbed.

4   Set a safety net. Create a safety statement for your
     protection.

5   Begin your induction.

Your 'safety net' statement is important in order to set clear
and precise boundaries of what you wish to accomplish in
trance. For example:

*I am going to go into trance for the next 20 minutes. During this
time I am going to 'X' in order to 'Y' (e.g. I am going to relax in
order to feel less anxious).*

*If during that time, anything should call into question my contin-
uing health and wellbeing, or if for any reason or emergency I
need to, I will immediately return to normal waking consciousness
with all the resources I need to effectively deal with the situation.*

*At the end of my 20-minute trance, I will awaken having accom-
plished my task with a sense of energy and refreshment.*

You are always ultimately in control of your experience.
Remember, no one has ever been unable to come out of a
trance. Going into trance and coming out are as natural as
sleeping and waking.

SYSTEMATIC RELAXATION

🔊) *You can download this audio technique now.*

Please read through this exercise before you do it and do not attempt it while driving or operating machinery. Only do it when it is safe and appropriate to do so.

Use your most comfortable, tired, drowsy voice to say each of the following to yourself as you follow the instructions below. Pause to notice your feelings once you have completed it, then, if you wish, you can repeat it. You will be able to return to full, waking consciousness, refreshed and alert, as soon as you are ready.

First, I want you to close your eyes and take a deep breath, letting go of stress as you exhale.

Now tell yourself the following:

Now I relax my eyes.

Now I relax my jaw.

Now I relax my tongue.

Now I relax my shoulders.

Now I relax my arms.

Now I relax my hands.

Now I relax my chest.

Now I relax my stomach.

Now I relax my thighs.

Now I relax my calves.

Now I relax my feet.

Now I relax my mind.

Once you have mastered the simple, systematic relaxation, let's try a more advanced self-hypnosis technique.

The Betty Erickson
self-hypnosis technique

It's time to learn the Rolls Royce of self-hypnosis. Even though it is still a relatively simple technique, it brings about a profound sense of relaxation. It quietens the incessant chitter chatter of people's minds and it is a really rich experience of the power of your imagination.

What many people don't know is Milton Erickson's wife Betty was very adept at self-hypnosis. Milton lived in Phoenix, Arizona, where he would often work on a patient in front of a group of gathered doctors, psychiatrists and psychologists. Milton was such a great hypnotist that even if you put on a video of him, (and I've done this a few times in seminars) the people watching it for educational purposes also get completely zoned out!

Milton liked to hypnotise everyone, including the experts who came to visit him. If someone did their best to resist him, then Betty would sometimes step in. She'd say: "I'd like to show you a technique that I use..." and because it wasn't Milton trying to hypnotise them, but instead it was a method of self-hypnosis, they were suddenly much more open to it. Her wonderful technique involves closing your eyes and describing three things you see, hear and feel – either in the real world or in your imagination. The reasoning behind it is, the more that you describe your internal world the more it alters your state from the experience of the external one.

THE 3, 2, 1 INDUCTION

🔊 *You can download this audio technique now.*

You are going to observe three things you can see, hear and feel, then two things and finally one thing. At any point, when you feel like closing your eyes, you describe the things internally that you can see, hear and feel. For example, whilst your eyes were open, you could say something like:

"Now I am aware that I can see the ceiling."

"Now I am aware that I can see a lamp."

"Now I am aware that I can see a chair."

continued

"Now I am aware that I hear traffic outside."

"Now I am aware that I hear the wind blowing."

"Now I am aware that I hear somebody walking."

"Now I am aware that I feel the chair supporting me."

"Now I am aware that I feel my breath."

"Now I am aware that I feel my eyelids blinking."

You then notice two things and then one. Remember, when you want to close your eyes, you then describe your internal images, sounds and feelings. This could be something like:

"Now I am aware that I see a beach."

"Now I am aware that I see the ocean."

"Now I am aware that I hear the ocean."

"Now I am aware that I hear people laughing."

"Now I am aware that I feel the sun on my body."

"Now I am aware that I feel the ocean lapping my feet."

Finally, you would describe one thing you see, one thing you hear and one thing you feel. Even though this is a simple process, if you lose your place and can't remember if it's visual or auditory next, that's perfectly fine, just keep describing your internal awareness, what you can see, hear and feel, because the more you describe your internal world, the richer it becomes and the deeper the trance experience will become. You may well notice your internal dialogue shuts off or you fall asleep and that's fine, too.

The process is simply this:

Three things you see.

Three things you hear.

continued

Three things you feel.

Two things you see.

Two things you hear.

Two things you feel.

One thing you see.

One thing you hear.

One thing you feel.

This process can help you feel really calm, using just the power of your imagination. You now might want to reinforce what you are doing by moving to the next stage.

Self-hypnosis through visualisation

By now you will be feeling more confident at using self-hypnosis and so it's time to move to the next step.

This visualisation technique is like the New Behaviour Generator as it installs deep relaxation by breaking it down into chunks. This is also my 'go to' method if I'm struggling to get back to sleep if I've woken up in the middle of the night.

This gets you to *'associate'* into a 'feel-good' picture and amplifies it over and over again so you boost positive feelings exponentially. Remember, by thinking *or* imagining anything, you affect your physiology, literally changing the chemistry and electricity in your body. So, if you think about going to the dentist, you remember there is a bit of discomfort involved, so you will go into a particular 'state'. If you walk down a dark alley at night and you hear footsteps behind you, your heartbeat will quicken, which is another 'state'. But if you remember a time when you were on holiday, or imagine what it would be like to be on a beach and you see, hear and feel all the things associated with that, again you change your 'state' to one of relaxation.

So, if I feel a bit worried, I close my eyes and relax, I imagine how I would look if I was twice as relaxed as I am right now. I make a picture of myself in my mind's eye as vividly as possible and then I float into that picture, seeing through the eyes of my more relaxed self, hearing my internal dialogue and feeling the greater relaxation. Then I do it again and again. By the third or fourth time, I feel terrific.

This has a cumulative effect – each time, you are stacking your feelings of relaxation and the feelings grow tremendously until you are completely blissed out!

NESTED IMAGES INDUCTION

🔊 *You can download this audio technique now.*

1. Imagine how you would look if you were twice as relaxed as you are right now.

2. Imagine floating into that more relaxed 'you'. See through the eyes of your more relaxed self, hear how it sounds and feel how it feels to be twice as relaxed.

3. From this place imagine how you would look if you were twice as relaxed again as you are right now.

4. Imagine floating into that more relaxed you. See through the eyes of your more relaxed self, hear how it sounds, and feel how it feels to be twice as relaxed.

5. From this place imagine how you would look if you were twice as relaxed once again as you are right now again.

continued

6 Imagine floating into that more relaxed you.
See through the eyes of your more relaxed self,
hear how it sounds, and feel how it feels to be
twice as relaxed.

By now you have the tools to create more calm,
resilience and happiness in your life.

Doing these techniques once is great. But the more
you practise them, the better you will get, and
you'll be able to tap into those fantastic feelings
whenever you need to.

Now it's time to bring all of the elements of this
guide together to create a richer world for yourself
and this is what we will focus on in the final section.

Section Three

Create a Richer World for Yourself

Now we've got your anxiety levels down and you are feeling more in control, let's empower you to make your world richer and return you to your natural setting of innate well-being and calmness on an on-going basis. We're going to do this using modern techniques from the realms of personal development.

They will help you to focus on what you *really* want, empower you to tap into the resources you have within yourself to achieve your goals and open your mind to living with a greater sense of 'self'. Whilst each technique in this section can be used in isolation, they can also be used cumulatively as one builds on the next.

Usually, when you sort out one aspect of your life other parts will slot into place too. A fascinating study done a few years ago found that people who were married tended to be happier. But when they observed the same couples over several years, they realised it wasn't about marriage at all. They discovered people who were happy formed happy relationships with other happy people – it was an inside/out job! I've also seen this time and time again with people I work with. Once they get in a better headspace, it's not just that they form functional relationships, but all aspects of their life flourish – from being motivated to start a business to relationships, and even improving their appearance.

One Californian life coach who helps women to boost their income discovered there was also an unexpected side effect to their success. As soon as they started to earn more money, they all lost weight so they felt even better about themselves! A human is an interdependent system, so if people fix one aspect of their life, then other things change for the better too.

Most people also don't spend their lives fully in the 'here and now'. Instead they worry endlessly about the past or what could happen in the future. Living more 'in the moment' doesn't take away the past or the ability to plan ahead, it just means you will get the best out of yourself each and every day – and it feels good!

Power questions

Historically, in our fast-paced world people rarely took the opportunity to catch a breath, listen to their inner self and ask big questions about their lives such as: What is my life's purpose? What do I truly want?

But ever since our world changed with the pandemic, I am asked more often, "What's the meaning of life?" A statement, often credited to Mahatma Gandhi, is: "You must be the change you wish to see in the world" – and in many ways that sentiment encompasses what this chapter is all about – as it's about changing yourself from the inside out in order to live a better life.

My firm belief is that there is no fixed meaning in life except the meaning you create. I have reached that conclusion after taking a lot of time to consider who I am, why I am here, and what my role is within the universe. The 'pause' of the pandemic's lockdowns, furlough, restrictions and working from home means more people than ever before are contemplating the bigger picture.

Inner personal development can empower you to feel good and live well. By this I'm not talking about embracing a new faith or religion. It's about moving away from a limited mode of thinking which is one of the reasons why so many people feel stressed out, unfulfilled or as if something is missing from their lives. Some people fill the void with drink, food, drugs, sex, shopping or work. Others sleepwalk through a lifetime. For some people that's enough – but others want more.

So if you are one of those people that wants more, in this section we are going to move beyond the boundaries of how you think about and see your 'self' and I am going to ask you to THINK BIG about who you really are and to look at your life with a different perspective – which includes a sense of higher self and purpose.

Opening your mind to new possibilities

Now you've reduced your anxiety you have much more headspace for other things – and there are so many exciting possibilities! Living a richer life means being open to opportunity. I have a sign that hangs on the door inside my closet that reminds me of this every day. It says:

"What would you do if you knew you couldn't fail?"

When I was still a radio DJ I asked myself that question and I decided: I'd be a hypnotist, I'd be on TV, I'd travel the world, I'd do shows, I'd work with all of the most amazing people in sport, the arts and business. I would live an exotic and wonderful life.

Then I asked myself: "Who would I need to become in order to make that happen?" I realised I'd have to educate myself further about hypnosis and psychology, be prepared to take a few risks (educated, calculated ones) and be prepared to fail. I'd even have to change the way I dressed, so I swapped my DJ uniform of T-shirt and jeans for suits.

I worked hard and all these things reinforced my new identity. But crucially I tried all of those new possibilities in my imagination first, outside the boundaries of who I thought I was and what I thought I could achieve.

We refer to the self-image (the way we see ourselves) as the blueprint for who we are. So, it's all of our possibilities, but it's also all of our limitations.

When I decided to take a calculated financial risk by putting on my first hypnotic show in London's West End I ran through all of the possibilities of what could go wrong – but also what could go right. The downside was I would take a hit financially and it would wipe out my savings but I'd still have a roof over my head. In the lead up to opening night, I was anxious about everything that could go wrong, thinking: "What if no-one shows up?" "What if I lose all my money?" But crucially I also worked through in my mind, the process of it all going brilliantly. I even took a photograph of myself outside the theatre with the 'House Full' sign, before the first ticket had been bought. I pinned it up in my kitchen, on a vision board I created, so I'd see it every day.

In some ways, the subconscious mind is a bit like a heat-seeking missile. If you give it a target, it will go for it. So, if you think continually about failing, you are feeding that potential into your unconscious mind and making it into a self-fulfilling prophecy. But you can do the same with success, too. The show the first week was about half full, it was almost full in the second, and by the third week every seat was sold out.

Becoming the ultimate you

The first technique in this section is designed to change your fixed and limited perception of your self. Anxious people see that state as a part of their identity – they think it is who they are. But now you aren't one of them, the whole point of visualisation and self-hypnosis is that you can start to discover the 'new you'. So anyone who thought they were anxious can now step outside of their old, familiar world of anxiety, where the world was threatening and they were constantly on a white knuckle ride.

I have created a technique based on the work of Byron Katie that can help your mind step outside of the limitations and boundaries we constrain ourselves with, in order to create new patterns of thinking.

When people ask me: "Why do you use hypnosis to achieve this?" the answer is simple. When you get comfortable and you visualise stuff you are literally giving yourself a chance of experiencing it in your mind before you do it for real in the outside world. It's like the old adage, measure the wood twice and cut it once. If I say to you, "Can you imagine what bacon-flavoured ice-cream would be like?" You'd put the two together in your mind and you might go, "Yuk!" or you might go, "Yum!". One of the amazing advantages that human beings have over animals is that we can imagine and design things inside our minds before we ever go about creating them in the real world.

The key to this thought experiment is to open up your imagination and think in terms of **possibility**. Then, when you rehearse and rehearse it, it begins to become a part of your new identity.

So, as you practise becoming a calmer, more optimistic and confident person, the world becomes a friendlier place too.

EXPERIENCING GREATER FREEDOM

🔊 *You can download this audio technique now.*

Read through this technique first so you fully understand it.

1   Make yourself comfortable.

2   Now ask yourself "Who would you be if it was impossible for you to get unnecessarily anxious no matter what?"

3   What would you feel and think like if you couldn't get unnecessarily anxious?

4   If you still experienced emotions, but for now anxiety was no longer there, who would you be and how would you feel if you were unable to experience unnecessary anxiety and stress, just for now, while we are doing this process?

5   In other words, if your protection mechanism still did all the good things it does for you, but stopped signalling as loud and as often, and for the next few minutes, as it goes into the background of your experience, who would you be now?

6   So, for the next few moments, allow it to move into the background of your experience even further.

7   And ask yourself, if it were impossible to experience unnecessary anxiety in this moment, who would you be? How would you feel? How would the world look?

8   How would your thoughts be different if it was impossible to have any unnecessary anxiety?

9   Now imagine that you cannot feel any unnecessary anxiety whatsoever and, in your mind, now live a day in your life. Go through

continued

the morning, afternoon and evening free of unnecessary anxiety and full of deep calm and feeling totally in control.

10 Now imagine that you cannot feel any unnecessary anxiety whatsoever and, in your mind, now live a *week* in your life.

11 Now imagine that you cannot feel any unnecessary anxiety whatsoever and, in your mind, now live a *year* in your life.

12 Now sit in this experience for at least another minute and do nothing as your emotional ecosystem and perceptual filters recalibrate to calmness.

Notice how you are more open to possibility and how your identity has begun to shift. You are no longer an anxious person, you are somebody that doesn't experience unnecessary anxiety.

Create a vision board
of success

I mentioned in the last chapter that one of my key philosophies in life is, "You get more of what you focus on." A practical way you can explore this is to create your own *vision board of success.*

The story goes when Michelangelo was asked how he managed to carve such a beautiful sculpture, he replied, "I saw the angel in the marble and carved until I set him free." That is the power of visualisation.

When I started out in my career in the '80s, I created my own vision board – as I firmly believe in manifestation and if you can dream it, you can potentially create it. If you look around you right now, pretty much everything you see will have once started as an idea in someone else's mind. My board included pictures of exotic places, a BMW I really wanted, cities I wanted to go to and, of course, the picture of me with a 'House Full' sign outside a theatre.

By creating the vision board, I told my unconscious mind, "Take my life in that direction!" I even got my bank statement and I cut the overdrawn bit out and I glued in a huge figure of tens of thousands of pounds in credit. I picked it up and I burst out laughing, as it felt so good!

A friend of mine at the time also made a vision board, as he wanted to be able to one day travel on Concorde. He wanted it so desperately he would pack his suitcase at the weekend, go to the airport and experience all the excitement and anticipation of travelling on the great plane, then, come home and watch a documentary video which was about flying on Concorde. A few weeks later, he got a job as an international radio correspondent – and his very first job was a flight on that aircraft. Even stranger was that on his vision board, he'd put a picture of a beautiful mountain village. One of his assignments was to go to Switzerland. When he arrived, he thought to himself, "This place looks familiar," and when he checked on his return, it was the exact same village that was pinned on his board!

How we organise our thinking, experience and behaviours

Anxious people often think: "I wish I worried less." Yet, sometimes change can seem hard or a bit daunting and so now I am going to guide you through another powerful process that can help. What I'm about to describe may seem complex, but by the time you finish reading through the entire process, it will all make sense.

Neurological Levels snaps you out of being 'stuck', gives you a structure in which to explore your new, richer world and helps you return to your natural setting of innate wellbeing and peace. It does this by opening you up to an *even greater* world of possibility. Take your time with this process as it can give you real insights.

There are six Neurological Levels made up of Environment, Behaviour, Beliefs, Values, Identity and the highest level Spirituality. As you move up, each level automatically changes the ones below it. So by going through them you can discover an answer to a problem – some people find it changes their entire life!

The key thing about Neurological Levels is that it gets you thinking about your life in terms of the *universal*. The world of people who are anxious is small and limited as it's survival focused and so they are stuck at the bottom level. Moving up through each level leads to a powerful process that flips this limited mind-set into a big, expansive one. Remember, even if you are sceptical about it just follow the process.

While it falls under the umbrella of spirituality, some aspects of Neurological Levels are grounded in hard science. It all started when social scientist and anthropologist Gregory Bateson created one of the original models used for NLP. Bateson was really into *systems* as a way of viewing the world. We could go into a very complex discussion here, but in simplified terms, 'systems' is all about the relationships of phenomena and the patterns that connect things. A good example of this is when a profit of a company is at a different level to the technology that creates the products and machines that make the packaging. Yet they are all part of the same *system*. There are systems everywhere, including companies, families and even human beings.

Bateson initially identified four levels of learning and changing as a mechanism in behavioural science. His work inspired Robert Dilts, who was one of the early pioneers of NLP, and who worked closely with NLP founders Richard Bandler and John Grinder. Dilts took Bateson's approach to systems and turned it into his own powerful NLP technique, adding further levels, and calling it Neurological Levels. You can only move *up* the levels to manifest change. What's also fascinating is that some scientists believe that when you get to the higher Neurological Levels of learning – including spirituality – you actually use more of your brain capacity!

Using the Neurological Levels

Always start at the first level of the hierarchy with **Environment.** This is all about where you are, who you are with and concentrates on concrete things you can see. People who are stuck at this bottom level (which includes anxious people) often feel they have no options. This manifests itself in the way they speak, as they will often say things such as: "I hate my job" or "I hate my boss". Often they complain about things in their environment as though they have no control over them and no power to change them. To free someone who is stuck we need to move out of environment up into the next levels so they can question themselves and find options or solutions. Before we actually do the technique, let me explain a little bit more about how it works.

Behaviour and Skills are the second and third levels. *What we do* is our behaviour. So if someone's environment is that their job is awful, they could explore other possibilities – and in doing so start to empower themselves. One way to change behaviour, for instance, is to consider if there are other opportunities in the workplace or even look for another job, and in so doing, create a better environment. Skills are about *how we do it*. So it's all about using your capabilities, talents and resources – or even training yourself with new skills to get to where you want to be. Open your mind to every possibility.

Values is the fourth level and this focuses on *why*. This is all about what is most important to a person, their beliefs, convictions and motivations. If someone forms a belief that something is possible they are more likely to get the skills and enact the behaviour necessary to get whatever they think is possible and that will change their environment too. If someone says: "I *can't*" they are usually right. This may seem surprising, but often people are unaware of their beliefs. So it's very important to get that crystal clear in your mind.

Sometimes people will have a conflicting belief. For instance, people may tell you: "I hate my job" but simultaneously when you ask them: "Why don't you leave?" they might answer: "I need the money." The 'need' is where they are stuck. I once helped a guy who said he had the most demoralising office job as his colleague's motto was: "Roll on, retirement!" It was sucking the life out of him but he felt trapped as he felt he 'needed' the salary that came with the role. The point of this exercise is to bust the story you are telling yourself. If you are telling yourself you can't leave this job as you need the money, that might be true right now. But if you need the money you might be able to find another job or another way of creating an income. This system is designed to get you to really question yourself – as at the fundamental level of 'stuckness' you will have created a rigid story that you may believe – but you need to push your boundaries and challenge yourself to get into possibility thinking outside of the limitation.

The fifth level is **Identity,** which is all about *who*. This is one of the most powerful areas for moving someone who is stuck. Identity beliefs tend to focus on 'I am' statements. So if someone, for instance, says: "I am a shy person" or "I am a talented person", that will affect all aspects of their life right down to environment. For example, if a person forms a belief about their identity that they are not a confident person, they will always prove that to be true. So use this opportunity to affirm positive aspects of your self.

Finally, the highest neurological level is **Spirituality.** The principle behind the top tier is that the universe is bigger than anything else i.e. Identity, Behaviours and so on. So ask yourself *"What is your mission or purpose in life?"* This empowers you as you are in touch with your spiritual self. Once someone ends up at 'Spirituality' there is often a Eureka moment – where they recognise their role in the wider universe. This means people can also gain key insights about themselves.

From time to time when I have a problem I use this process. Recently, I was one of the key speakers at a major event and I felt under time pressure. I went for coffee with a friend who is also an NLP trainer and he said: "How are you?" I admitted: "I've got a *lot* to do in the next few days and I'm starting to think how on earth am I going to get through it!" He said: "Why don't you do Neurological Levels?" He talked me through each stage, starting with: "What is the environment?" Which was a conference room. Then he moved up a level to my behaviour, asking "What do you believe?" My answer was: "There's a heck of a lot to get done!" Next he moved on to my abilities, asking me: "What are your resources?" My answer was: "I've trained for decades!" My identity led me to the answer: "I'm skilled at helping others." And when we moved into the spiritual level I reminded myself I believe my life's purpose is to make a positive difference and enrich people's lives. By the end of the process I'd moved out of anxiety mode and back into my 'can do' mindset, I knuckled down and I nailed it. We can all get bogged down in the small stuff from time to time, but when you move your thought processes into the 'big picture' it puts things into perspective. So lets put it into action.

NEUROLOGICAL LEVELS

Read through this technique first, then download the audio track. 🔊

I would like you to pick a problem that is troubling you. Then ask yourself the questions and when you have the answer go up into the next level. See what the outcome is, once your have worked up through every stage. Remember to keep an open mind.

Even though some people like to write everything down, in this particular case, please download the audio and let me walk you through it.

Environment

Your environment is *where* you are, with whom, concrete things that you can perceive.

So, ask yourself, where does the problem you want to solve, happen or exist?

Behaviour

What we do is our behaviour. For example, if your environment is that your job is awful, you can look for another job, and that new behaviour will create a new environment.

So, ask yourself, what new behaviour can you generate around your problem?

Skills

How can you change things? Consider your capabilities, talents and resources. So, if your job is awful you can summon determination to find another job, or you can learn techniques to make you motivated to make changes in your work environment so you can enjoy it.

So, ask yourself, what skills, talents and resources do I currently have, or what new skills can I learn?

continued

Values

Why are you here in this situation? Your values are the things that are most important to you, they are in a sense your deepest beliefs and convictions. So, there are several ways to answer the above question. It could be as simple as "I'm in this situation because even though I don't like my job, I still have to pay the bills." Therefore, paying my bills is more important to me, and it is because it gives me a sense of security. So, the underlying value here is 'security'. Often people are unaware of what their underlying beliefs really are. Get clear about yours so you can properly work through them.

So, ask yourself, why am I in this situation and what's ultimately most important to me?

Identity

Who are you? What is your mission or purpose in life? This is one of the most powerful areas for moving someone who is stuck. Identity statements tend to be 'I am' statements. How you perceive yourself affects everything about you.

So, ask yourself, who am I?

Spirituality

At the highest neurological level ask yourself, "Why am I here in the Universe?". The Universe is bigger than anything, identity, beliefs, etc. So, for a universal perspective everything is affected. Your mission in life contains the most power.

So, ask yourself, why am I here in this life?

Living a richer life

Today I try to live my life in a universal sense – as that gives me a sense of purpose and drives me to make a positive difference to people's lives. Spirituality and religion are two different things. I have explored many faiths through my life although I now choose to be a Zen Buddhist. I consciously create as much joy in every single moment that I can. I experience a rich tapestry of emotions all day long, but it's not without any sense of value or purpose. I am very much a work in progress! And I am pragmatic about religion – if it works for you that is great.

But one thing mindfully exploring your place in the universe can achieve is to help you to crystallise what your priorities are. While we all need to pay the bills, trying to find a healthy balance is key to a richer life.

Genpo Roshi some years ago came to stay at my house in LA, shortly after we'd first met. At that point I was so driven in my career that I'd launch out of bed firing on all cylinders and work relentlessly every day. When Genpo came down in the morning, I'd already been busy for hours. So over breakfast chitchat, assuming he'd been sat in the Zazen (or Lotus) position for hours, I said: "What have you been doing this morning? Meditating?" He said: "No." I then asked: "So have you been *contemplating* then?" Yet again he said: "No." Then he gave me an important life lesson. He told me: "I have noticed you are all about *doing* stuff and *having* stuff, but you are not very much into *being*."

He recognised I was into 'doing' and 'having' as I was in LA, the land of the over-achiever! But I had neglected that other part of my self. His words stopped me and I said: "Thank you for that insight." I considered what he had told me and it confirmed in my mind I didn't have to get up, attack the day, compete with everyone else and pursue more 'stuff' as there would never be an end to it. I'd already been looking at making changes to my life and it helped me to realise I needed more balance. It wasn't long after that I left LA.

Spiritual teacher Eckhart Tolle in his book *The Power Of Now* says: "All negativity is caused by an accumulation of psychological time and denial of the present. Unease, anxiety, tension, stress, worry – all forms of fear – are caused by too much future, and not enough presence. Guilt, regret, resentment, grievances, sadness, bitterness and all forms of non-forgiveness are caused by too much past, and not enough presence."

So, the gist of what he's saying is that if you're spending too much time thinking about the past, or worrying about the future, then, you're denying yourself the beauty and joy of the present.

People often say things like: "It's alright for them, they're wealthy so of course they are happy." But many models and multi-millionaires I have met had material wealth and success yet they were deeply unhappy people as they were constantly anxious about their appearance or accruing more and more.

I was once told a version of a famous Chinese saying that I feels sums it up: 'If you want to be happy for an hour take a nap, if you want to be happy for a week go on holiday, if you want to be happy for a year, win the lottery, if you want to be happy for the rest of your life help other people.'

Taking a universal perspective on your life will give you a roadmap for living that supports your goals.

The mind-set of a functional life

I cannot emphasise enough the importance of a positive mind-set as being key to living a functional, purposeful and richer life.

NLP Master Trainer Michael Breen, 30 years ago modelled the thought processes of Vic Charles MBE – one of the most accomplished martial artists in the world. He told me Vic is one of the most extraordinarily positive guys he had ever met. When I asked Michael, "What's Vic's core strategy?", he said he has a powerful process of continual positive reinforcement. So if he arrives at the airport on time it's a win, if he's enjoying his breakfast, it's a win. He is continually creating stronger neural networks in his brain that reinforce his self-image as a winner. That super positive mind-set led him to become an 8th Dan Black Belt, a winner of multiple World Championships, and he was even described by one of his opponents as "the greatest competitor he had ever seen". He was even awarded an MBE for services to karate.

Anxious people are reinforcing the idea that the world isn't safe and that there are threats everywhere. Vic Charles is reinforcing opportunity and success in every small thing he does. What that does is it shapes his perceptual filters so he sees the world as one great big opportunity and place to succeed. He literally has a winner's mind-set! Not only does this put him in a great state of mind and body but his emotional energy will be something that everyone picks up on and will attract *even more* good energy too.

By continually listening to and practising the techniques in written or audio form in this book, you will also give yourself a mind-set for success. You will train your brain to develop a positive mind-set of perceptual filters that sorts for happiness and success.

Hindsight ahead of time

Now, for our penultimate exercise, we are going to head off into the distant future, towards the end of your lifetime and imagine that you have had the best life ever.

We are going to figure out what made your life so brilliant and bring that insight back to the 'here and now.' So, you will have the benefit of hindsight ahead of time in order to create a roadmap for creating the best possible life for yourself from this moment forward.

I have done this myself and it gave me insights about how I want to live. In my mind's eye I worked through the assumption I had enjoyed the most fabulous life ever. And then I reverse engineered in my mind all the major events that would have had to happen for me to experience such a brilliant life – looking at health, family, career, etc.

With hindsight ahead of time, you can incorporate as much of your dreams as you can into your 'here and now.' You can check in with yourself to see how well you are doing and how focused on your purpose you are. You can use this as a barometer to see if you are living your best life.

We are going to do this process through the guided meditation audio technique that accompanies this book.

🔊 *Please download the track **Hindsight Ahead of Time** now.*

Harnessing the power of your conscious and unconscious mind through trance

Finally, I want to draw your attention to the other benefits of the main hypnotic trance that comes with this book.

Embedded in the trance is my version of The Big Mind Technique, which is, I believe, the finest meditation in the world. Created by Genpo Roshi, it expands your consciousness and sense of who you are. This will give you an even richer world perspective.

But first, I want to explain to you why the trance is such a powerful tool and how it works. While you can consciously try to change your life, hypnosis, imagination and visualisation are all powerful ways of communicating directly with the unconscious mind, which drives all of our thoughts and behaviours.

Using trance is one of the most effective ways of talking to the unconscious. The conscious mind is the mind we actively think with and it is the little voice inside our head. It thinks in a linear fashion, conceptualising and categorising information. It can only hold a handful of ideas at any one time, it is critical and analytical and it sorts information by noticing differences.

The unconscious, or subconscious mind, is the larger mind and it contains all of our wisdom, memories and intelligence. It is our source of creativity, regulates body maintenance and autonomic processes like breathing, blood circulation and tissue regeneration. It is the seat of the emotions and directs nearly all of our behaviour. Everything that has ever happened to us, or everything we have ever imagined, is stored as a multi-sensory recording in the unconscious mind. You can use hypnosis to tap into the unconscious, or larger mind, which works by association – it looks at, and sees similarities with past events.

The words 'conscious' and 'unconscious' are models for the way our mind operates. Being conscious or unconscious is actually a spectrum of awareness, rather than a fixed point.

The best way to describe it is if you imagine a darkened room with objects littered about it, the conscious mind is like a torch, which picks out only details in the room. It can only focus on a few things at any one time. Whatever the torch is shining upon will be brightly lit and visible, while the rest of the room will be dark – although it is still there. You may not be able to see it but it definitely exists. Whatever your attention is focused on (i.e. the beam of light is shining on) is uppermost in your conscious and the rest of your memories and wisdom are still there, but they are in the dark bit of the room.

While we are largely unaware of our autonomic processes, every single minute our unconscious mind is receiving countless messages through sensory awareness that make things happen inside our bodies. They normally don't trouble our conscious mind as we would not be able to process them all without getting overwhelmed.

A simple metaphor for this is, imagine you are at a party where there are lot of people talking all around you. All the while your unconscious mind is listening to all those conversations simultaneously. That means if someone says your name over the other side of the room, suddenly you tune in to that conversation and it becomes a part of your consciousness.

That same mechanism can be used through trance to install some positive software in your mind.

The left and right brain

As well as the unconscious and conscious, the human brain is divided into a 'left brain' and a 'right brain'. The 'left brain' is the domain of logical, linear and sequential thinking, while the right is associative, abstract and emotive.

The conscious narrative in this book is talking to the 'left brain', the visualisation exercises are communicating with the 'right brain' and when we use hypnosis we are talking to the whole brain simultaneously.

Our western culture is dominated by the 'left brain' with a big emphasis on logic and structure. But to operate optimally as human beings, we need to also engage the right. Scientists now believe that true intelligence is defined not by right or left brain dominance, but the interplay between the two.

As you listen to the trance that goes with this book, messages in the right ear go straight to the left brain which likes to process instruction. So I will tell it to do things like relax, or feel better, become calm – using simple, direct commands.

The right brain likes metaphor and 'the abstract' and so you will hear stories that are about becoming more resilient, optimistic or overcoming adversity, which leads to a more sophisticated way of communicating with your whole brain.

The Big Mind Technique

My version of Genpo Roshi's Big Mind Technique takes you to an expanded state of consciousness, in a similar way to Dilt's Neurological Levels in order to open your mind even further.

The aim is to transform everything including your beliefs, your identity and your behaviours, no matter the situation. Who we *think* we are is what Genpo calls 'The Small Mind' and it's made up of (and limited by) our thoughts, beliefs and ideas. Big Mind is an expanded consciousness in which our worries, fears and anxieties transform.

Big Mind gets you to explore different aspects of your 'self', which can include 'protector', 'evaluator', and 'controller'. Through the meditation you can ask these parts of your identity to disappear into the background of your experience. This demonstrates that you don't have to be limited in your ways of thinking about who you are. Once you are in a state of expanded consciousness, there is no sense of your limitations, and you can experience a richer life.

When you expand your consciousness through trance, your worries, fears and anxieties dissipate.

For some, just one listen of it will have a massive impact. For others repeated use of the trance has a cumulative effect over time. Either way, listen to it as often as you need to.

Your better life...

My greatest hope from you using this system is not only has your anxiety significantly reduced, but also you see a greater world of possibility and you are filled with more optimism and joy than you ever dreamed possible before.

Until we meet...

Paul McKenna

Index of Techniques

The Hypnotic Trance

SECTION ONE

SECTION TWO

SECTION THREE

Acknowledgements

I would like to thank the following people: Caroline Michel, Beth Bishop, Wayne Davies, Marcus Leaver, Michael Neill, Michael Breen, Alex Tuppen, Neil Reading, Steve Shaw, Ben Hasler, Kate McKenna and Mike Osborne for all their efforts on this project.

A very special thanks to Sarah Arnold.

Notes

Notes

Notes

Notes

Notes